New York

in the Progressive Era

NEW YORK
IN THE PROGRESSIVE ERA

Social Reforms and Cultural Upheaval, 1890–1920

PAUL M. KAPLAN

THE
History
PRESS

Published by The History Press
Charleston, SC
www.historypress.com

First published 2021

Manufactured in the United States

ISBN 9781467143486

Library of Congress Control Number: 2020948650

For three close friends—Sharon Goldman, who educates; Josh Brook, who writes plays; and Jacob Koskimaki, who composes songs and novels.

New York at Sunrise

By Anna Hempstead Branch

When with her clouds the early dawn illumes
Our doubtful streets, wistful they grow and mild;
As if a sleeping soul grew happy and smiled,
The whole city radiantly blooms.
Pale spires lift their hands above the glooms
Like a resurrection, delicately wild,
And flushed with slumber like a little child,
Under a mist, shines forth the innocent Tombs.
Thus have I seen it from a casement high,
As unsubstantial as a dream it grows.
Is this Manhattan, virginal and shy,
That in a cloud so rapturously glows?
Ethereal, frail, and like an opening rose,
I see my city with an enlightened eye.

Anna Hempstead Branch worked as a settlement house worker in New York City's Lower East Side during the Progressive Era. Her poem depicts the hope from a multitude of reforms enacted during this period.

CONTENTS

CONTENTS

How This Book Works

This book pieces together the main movements of the Progressive Era (1890–1920), showing the profound societal changes sweeping the United States, with an emphasis on New York State.

The first section, The Decades Before the Progressive Era, describes the factors that led to the Progressive Era. Rapid industrialization, unprecedented immigration offering cheap labor and rapid technological advancement helped created an extremely wealthy class. With a demand for more office and technical work, a middle class emerged. This new class would reshape the values, leisure and morals of the day. Middle-class women would become more educated and marry later. Some were demanding societal changes.

But the poor and working-class felt left behind. The economy was shifting in an uncomfortable way from smaller firms serving their communities to larger corporations. In the 1870s and 1880s, there was dissent in the air in the United States and especially in bustling New York State. From these shifts, reformers rallied for improvements in housing, conservation, labor conditions, racial rights, women's suffrage and much more.

The remainder of the book describes these changes that occurred during the Progressive Era, encompassing three areas: social reform, anti-monopoly and organizational efficiency. The book describes national changes through the lens of New York State.

Each area of reform is grouped as a part or larger theme. Within each part, various chapters illustrate examples.

The following timeline shows key events during this period.

April 9, 1865
Civil War ends with Robert E. Lee's surrender at Appomattox Court House, Virginia

May 10, 1869
Transcontinental Railroad is completed

Early 1870s
Gilded Age begins

1890–1920
Progressive Era

April 1901
Tenement House Act passed in New York State Legislature

February 1913
Ratification of Sixteenth Amendment, allowing for personal income tax

January 1914
Gilded Age ends with Henry Ford paying workers five dollars a day at Ford Motor Company in Dearborn, Michigan

January 1920
Prohibition goes into effect

August 1920
Ratification of Nineteenth Amendment for women's suffrage

October 24, 1929
Stock market starts its crash when richest Americans lose substantial wealth.*

* Some historians consider the stock market crash to mark the true end of the Gilded Age.

ACKNOWLEDGEMENTS

Thanks to the following venues for their research materials and reference services: the staff at the Yale Club of New York, including Christina Kasman; the New York Society Library, including Carolyn Waters; the Library of Congress, Division of Prints & Photographs; and the Poets House downtown for helping me select a suitable poem. Thanks to the Henry Ford Museum and Ford Piquette for providing research opportunities. I also acknowledge the contributions of authors and academics of previous books, articles and documentaries on this subject, who are noted in the bibliography. Thanks also to Eileen Kaplan for her editing and content suggestions.

A shout-out to Banks Smither, editor at Arcadia Publishing and The History Press, and the press's publicists and sales staff.

I also thank key venues for book talks, including the Harvard Club, Yale Club, Union League of New York, General Society Library, Jewish Museum of Florida, Lower East Side Jewish Conservancy, Museum at Eldridge Street and many more. Also, thanks to *Writer's Voice* for this fine radio show's support of my other book projects.

I also nod to the support of friends and family, including Jack and Eileen Kaplan; brother Andrew and Leo and Aquarius Kaplan; Uncle Ted Katz, who brainstormed titles for the book; Karen, Deha, Kyle and Julian Rozanes; Diane, Ed, Mango and Willow Ziegman; and Robert and Jane Katz. Friends not already mentioned who provided encouragement on this project include Christine Allers, Barney Pearson, Daphne Balick, Jiyoung Cha, Alfred Robert Hogan, Ron Klayman, Matus Kopunec, Bonnie Kintzer, Yan Ma, Angela Pruitt, Karen Seiger and Felix and Gracie Kaplan.

INTRODUCTION

In the closing decades of the nineteenth century in New York State, profound change was coming. The Gilded Age had produced great income disparity. What were once agrarian and rural communities were rapidly transforming into urban centers. Industrialization was changing the lives of New York State residents. Suddenly, electricity lit up their streets; travelers were taking trolley cars and early prototypes of the automobile, rather than relying on horses; and buildings in New York City began to reach the sky. The bustling metropolis's population was on its way to becoming one of the most influential cities in the world.

Many social classes felt left in the dust of this rapid-fire transformation. Rugged individualism and minimalist, laissez-faire government were bedrock principles of the barely one-century-old nation. But some reformers began to challenge these government hands-off policies. The working class was laboring in often dangerous jobs with no protections. Women could not vote and did not have much of a voice in government. Housing in crowded neighborhoods, like the Lower East Side, was unsanitary and hazardous for the immigrant families who rented them. In rural New York, land was being bought up and developed, often trampling on parks and forests. At the same time, many industries were engaging in illegal behavior by forming monopolies with unfair advantages over smaller players and receiving kickbacks and bribes. New York City and State governments were steeped in corruption.

Introduction

The Progressive Era (1890–1920) ushered in a wave of cultural, political and societal changes. Three themes that defined the Progressive Era were the common good, anti-monopolism and organizational efficiency.

Of these, the most profound was the common good. It was a shift in societal thinking. No longer could the public blame the poor for their circumstances or believe that the government should not provide basic protections for workers—or that landlords could rent apartments in any condition. The new idea was that reformers, clergy, responsible businesspeople and lawmakers needed to improve society.

Reformers advocated for a variety of changes to business, government and households. These reforms included housing improvements, public health, labor rights, antitrust legislation, personal income tax, women's suffrage, "scientific management" of industry and prohibition. Such calls for change came from many corners of society: the middle class, with its increased educational access; Protestant ministers preaching a social gospel; reformers seeking to change housing and labor laws; and reporters, who sought to document injustices to bring awareness to often overlooked groups. Activists also innovated with new types of solutions like settlement houses, where social service, health care or education workers moved into the neighborhoods they serviced.

But while the Progressive Era saw gains in many of these areas, it also overreached into people's lives. Reformers and ministers formed an unlikely alliance to bring about the passage of Prohibition. Many resented being told what to drink or how to spend their leisure time. In other ways, reformers fell short. Unions were useful for protecting workers, but many discriminated against Black people, women and unskilled workers. White women reformers were focused on gaining the vote but did little to help Black women achieve the same right. That fell largely to Black leaders, journalists and ministers. Progressives also had a dark side, with many advocating eugenics. Others valued organizational efficiency to a detriment, with programs like Frederick Taylor's scientific management, which treated workers like cogs in an assembly line to be optimized. It never caught on.

Former New York governor and president Theodore Roosevelt tried to bust illegal monopolies and trusts. He also curtailed the common practice of kickbacks. Besides trying to even the business playing field, he was also the father of the modern conservation movement in his effort to preserve forests, parks and endangered species.

This book looks at the forces behind the Progressive Era—why it took off and why it ultimately ended in 1920. It brings forth several overlooked activists from history, including the suffragents, men who helped pass the Nineteenth Amendment; the ground-breaking public relations tactics of the anti-saloon league for Prohibition's passage; the contrasting philosophies among Black leaders and scholars on how to achieve equal rights; and the passage of the income tax to compensate for the loss of the excise tax on alcohol during efforts to pass Prohibition. While the focus is the Progressive Era in New York State, the book describes much about national trends to show the backdrop. All of the national trends were mirrored in both urban and rural New York.

A surprising number of questions raised during the Progressive Era echo in present-day newspapers. What are just immigration laws? How does the United States balance its needs versus providing a safe haven for refugees? What is the appropriate minimum wage? Should marijuana be legalized and permitted to be sold in retail outlets? How can conservationists effectively preserve the environment despite developers' objections? How can poor urban and rural areas be improved? How can big tech companies be broken up if they are unfairly crowding out smaller players? How can organizations be more efficient in making data-based decisions?

All of these questions were posed by people in the late nineteenth century. The setting and context were different, but the core questions remain. In looking back at this period, we see foreshadowing of the future.

Enjoy the book.

Part I

DECADES BEFORE THE PROGRESSIVE ERA

DISSENT IS IN THE AIR
IN 1870S AND '80S NEW YORK

A t the conclusion of the Civil War, the damage to the nation was enormous. Abraham Lincoln spoke of "binding up the nation's wounds," but the loss of life was devastating. Southern cities lay in ashes. Factories and farms lay in ruin. It also unleashed an enormous sweep of social, political and economic change. About four million formerly enslaved people were now considered free. The federal government borrowed extensively. In 1860, the federal budget was $78 million, and in 1865, the budget was $1.3 billion. By 1867, after the war had ended, the budget shrank to $377 million but was still five times the size of the budget before the Civil War.[1]

The end of the Civil War gave rise to rapid industrialization and manufacturing. The time became known as the Gilded Age, a term that comes from *The Gilded Age: The Tale of Today* by Mark Twain and Charles Warner, which depicts the corruption. The phrase was brilliant for capturing the duality of the time. Like a gilded piece of jewelry that looks like solid gold but underneath lies black steel, so too was this age. On the one hand, it was a time of great expansion as society rapidly changed from agricultural to industrial. But it was also a time of great income inequality, and strikes challenged the vision of great progress. Walt Whitman encapsulated many of these fears, stating, "If the United States, like the countries of the Old World, is also to grow vast crops of poor, desperate, dissatisfied, nomadic, miserably-waged populations…then our republican experiment, notwithstanding its surface successes is at heart an unhealthy failure."

1870–90: The Rise of the Gilded Age in New York

The Gilded Age saw a tremendous expansion of industry, which fueled the new super-rich classes with household names like Vanderbilt and Rockefeller. Many wrestled with the question of whether they were captains of industry or robber barons. Many Americans began to see the Gilded Age as a time of worker exploitation, political corruption, urban crisis and rising income equality. In response, radicals and reformers emerged and pushed through dramatic changes. These so-called progressives included journalists, politicians, social workers, labor activists and women's rights activists. There was also a category often overlooked—Protestant ministers. All of these groups believed the excesses of the Gilded Age called for great reforms. They rejected the laissez-faire government and individualism, believing that government and activist individuals could reform society and focus on the common good.

The nation's population was exploding. In 1860, there were only thirty-one million Americans. In subsequent decades, though, population growth was exponential. Americans were moving in large numbers from farms to cities. While these cities offered more excitement and job opportunities for some, they also had high rates of crime, disease and unrest. Some believed that rapid urbanization threatened the nation's bedrock values.

These changes were occurring on a national level but were especially apparent in New York State. Indeed, the rise of the middle class, the influx of immigrants and the accumulation of wealth by the upper rich was reconfiguring New York's class structure. The middle class began to separate from the labor-toiling and the upper rich. This budding class brought distinct forms of work, consumption, clothing, leisure and values. It brought a new role for women in particular. Many in the middle class married later and had fewer children than did their working-class or newly arrived immigrant counterparts. Some entered the workplace, though most would leave their jobs after bearing children. More went to college. Many also started to demand changes, such as the right to vote.

Progressives enacted policies to rein in big business, improve public health, provide greater opportunity, preserve the environment and decrease income inequality. The Gilded Age's income inequality in New York City was personified by the opulent mansions on Fifth Avenue versus the notorious slums of Five Points and the ultra-crowded Lower East Side neighborhoods.

Spurred by the Industrial Revolution, the United States had enjoyed precipitous growth in population, wealth and technological advancement. It shook society in ways few could have imagined.

During the 1870s and 1880s, social classes were separated by a wide gulf. In New York City, the haves and have nots were living in what seemed like different universes. The most prosperous families were wealthy capitalists: financiers, landowners, executives, some manufacturers and families with inherited wealth. Comprising about 1 percent of the country, this elite group had completely different lives from wage workers and farmers. They controlled much of society's resources and disproportionately influenced politics. This group included about four thousand millionaires. At the top of this heap were about two hundred families worth a staggering $20 million or more. They tended to be concentrated in the Northeast, with many in New York State. Some of these families are still household names: Vanderbilt, Whitney, Carnegie, Rockefeller and Morgan. Most were of English descent, were Protestant (Episcopalian, Presbyterian or Congregational) and came from affluent families. Generally, social classes were not fluid. However, there were notable exceptions, like Scottish immigrant Andrew Carnegie and John Rockefeller, who came from a poor family in upstate New York.

Industrialists like Carnegie and Rockefeller tended to believe in steadfast individualism. Through hard work, they reasoned, anyone could pull himself up. Andrew Carnegie, echoing the sentiments of many in this circle, discussed how exceptional leaders must be able to spread their wings. His *Gospel of Wealth* noted, "It is the leaders who do the new things that count. All these have individualist tendencies to a degree beyond ordinary means and worked in perfect freedom. Each and every one a character unlike anybody else; an original, gifted beyond most others of his kind, hence his leadership."[2] There was a certain idealism—and naiveté—to the philosophy. No matter what circumstance one was from, he or she could elevate to a higher position. It supposed that the system was a level playing field.

Many in New York State agreed with this philosophy, including those in the working class. They prized the self-made man. Most had come from faraway lands with big dreams and ambitions. Some saw the industrialists as men who had made the most of their resources and showed great business acumen. Many aspired to be like them.

An Irish immigrant, James Murray, lived in New York City and wrote a letter to his family in Ireland, expounding the virtues of the self-made man: "Read this letter…and tell all the poor Folk of your Place, the God has opened a Door for their Deliverance; for here is no scant of Bread.…You may get Land here for 10 pounds a Hundred Acres....There are servants come here out of Ireland, who have served their time here, who are now Justices of the Peace."

Horatio Alger's 1868 novel, *Ragged Dick*, tells the story of a young boy who earned his living as an orphan. The transformation begins with opening a savings account and learning to read. Through hard work and seizing opportunities, he grows into a middle-class existence. The values the popular novel instilled lasted for decades. Individuals could improve their lot. Anyone could be rich—or at least respectable. Everyone's backyard, it was said, was filled with diamonds.

Rags to riches stories were popular among New Yorkers. Even those born into wealth presented themselves as self-made. Teddy Roosevelt was a prime example. He claimed that his physical regimen that transformed his feeble body as a youth during the 1860s and '70s was an illustration of how he overcame obstacles.

At its extreme, this philosophy was Social Darwinism. Some could not adapt to their circumstances and therefore, did not deserve a successful life. This philosophy stood in stark contrast to those who said the poor were largely the victims of circumstances. Social Darwinism, though, argued that poor people were doomed to their struggles by nature.

BACKLASH TO SOCIAL DARWINISM AND RUGGED INDIVIDUALISM

Large industrialists, for the most part, embraced Social Darwinism. Social reformers, unsurprisingly, did not. Workers and farmers began to point fingers at politicians, Wall Street and big business. They noted that poverty was caused by poor housing conditions, poor education and a lack of health care. This backlash underscored some of the aims of the reformers. They asked, "Why wasn't everyone benefitting from the industrial revolution?"

Henry George's best-selling 1879 book, *Progress and Poverty*, called attention to the large income gulf endemic in New York: "It is as though an immense wedge were being forced, not underneath society, but through society. Those who are above the point of separation are elevated, but those who are below are crushed down."

He lamented the rising monopoly power. The rich were becoming richer. It was, in effect, the new American aristocracy. He warned that this threatened the well-being of the nation.

Church leaders agreed with his assessment. Many ministers saw massive income inequality as unstable for society. One example was Episcopal pastor William Rainsford. He warned his congregation, "Never were the lines between the two classes—those who have wealth and those who envy them—more distinctly drawn. Elaborate and costly manifestations of wealth would only tend to stir up widespread discontent and furnish additional texts for sermons by the socialistic agitators."[3] His warning was clear: discontent was brewing, and the ultra-rich who comprised some of his congregation needed to think twice before flaunting their wealth. Underlying the quote is a veiled threat of agitation from discontented masses struggling to get by.

Essayist Jackson Lears at the Gilder-Lehrman Institute of American History explains these differing views:

> *Moralists tended to overlook the contradictory impact of monopoly power. They also ignored the speculative aspects of money, which they treated not as a manipulating instrument of power but a just reward for hard work. The poor, from this view, were responsible for their own plight. Visions of self-made manhood proliferated, promoted by such self-help writers as Horatio Alger. Such "boys" books traced the rise of bootblacks to bank clerks, and Russell Conwell, the Baptist minister who declared "Acres of Diamonds" to be the proper reward of the hard-working Christian.*
>
> *Working-class folk were not impressed. They knew that pulling yourself up by your bootstraps was trickier than any self-help writer imagined. That was why they embraced an ethic of solidarity rather than individualist striving. Solidarity took institutional form in the labor unions that miners, railroad laborers, and other skilled industrial workers organized to protect themselves against their employers' relentless drive to maximize profits through maximum productivity—which meant squeezing as much work out of their labor force for as little pay as possible.[4]*

The poorer classes themselves also tended to take a dim view of their own poverty. Some saw poverty as the will of God. Their emphasis was on leading a righteous—if indigent—life to prepare for the more important afterlife. Others saw poverty as a result of their own shortcomings. Furthermore, "much of the public also believed poverty was a necessary and expected human condition. They did not see a real reason to change it. In fact, many doubted whether change would even be possible."[5] Compounding the problem were corrupt bureaucrats who took bribes to look the other way when reformers tried to enforce anti-poverty laws.

ROLE OF WOMEN AND CHILDREN
DURING THE GILDED AGE

Women's roles as earners for the family varied markedly between classes. Upper classes tended to look down on working women. They were concerned that women working would upend the traditional family structure. But working-class families usually had to rely on two wages. Working-class women before marriage often toiled in textile mills, garment shops, restaurants or homes. After marriage and/or childbirth, these women often continued to contribute to the household income from work-at-home jobs like making artificial flowers, sewing dresses or providing for boarders who offset rents.

Children were often expected to bring in money for the families, as well. Some were pulled out of school to support their families. Education was often seen as a luxury. Sometimes, parents encouraged their children to cheat on physical tests measuring their competency for work. For example, for jobs requiring a minimum weight, children sometimes put a weight in their pocket to meet the requirement.

Children were also exploited greatly in terms of the dangers they were exposed to, long hours and grueling labor. Laws were enacted to protect children. However, they were often not enforced or were foiled by employers. One trick factory owners played was raising the U.S. flag on an outside flagpole when inspectors arrived, under the pretense of patriotism. The concealed purpose was to alert all children in the factory to go home for the day.

Newsies were often teenage boys, and sometimes girls, sauntering the streets selling newspapers. They were known for calling out headlines to entice customers to buy the papers. They usually paid the publishers for the papers and sold copies. Any unsold copies could not be returned. Though as a result of the newsboy strike of 1899, some publishers reluctantly agreed to concessions like accepting unsold copies. Boys also worked as peddlers, junkers and, illicitly, in gangs.

Teenagers of poor households sometimes saw themselves as burdens on their families. As a result, some would leave home. From their standpoint, they were then less of a drain on family resources. The famed composer Irving Berlin, for example, left his home on Cherry Street in the impoverished Lower East Side not long after his father died. He saw himself as a burden to his family. He became a newsie and a busker, a low-wage musical job for teenagers. A music producer would hire a busker to learn a song by heart

Above: Mary Malchade, 27 Roosevelt Street, nine years old, sells newspapers near the Brooklyn Bridge in New York City in 1909. Newsies suffered harsh working conditions. *Lewis Hine, Library of Congress, Prints and Photographs Division.*

Left: Two kids sell newspapers in 1910 outside the entrance of a saloon. Photo taken as part of National Child Labor Committee. *Library of Congress, Prints and Photographs Division.*

and sing it in cafés and on street corners. The business objective was to entice audiences to go see a show or buy sheet music.

Girls tended to work in garment factories or helping their mothers with childcare, cleaning and paying boarders. Most kids dutifully gave their wages to their parents. For economic and social reasons, they tended to live at home longer than their middle- and upper-class peers. Many of these low-income households in New York consisted of immigrants who arrived in the United States with the value of family economy. This meant that each member of the family, under the father's watchful eye, contributed his or her earnings for the benefit of the entire family. Many did not see this as a burden per se. Rather, they viewed this familial arrangement as necessary for survival. According to Judith Smith, "At every step of the way—from Europe to America, from the country to the city, from childhood to adulthood, workers knew that these strong mutual ties made life possible in America."[6]

Urban Problems in New York in the Mid- to Late Nineteenth Century

Income inequality and dangerous working conditions were only part of the bustling metropolis of New York's problems. As the city grew, its social problems were exacerbated. Crime, fire, disease, corruption and crowded housing were among them. Riots were becoming more violent and deadly. Poverty was one cause of this. Some turned to illicit ways of earning or drinking heavily, which sometimes yielded more crime. The police force was generally poorly trained and lightly armed. In essence, eighteenth-century police enforcement was trying to counter nineteenth-century crime. Realizing a need, New York City officials abolished the night watch and established a paid and professional police force, requiring the carrying of weapons and wearing of uniforms.

Fires were also a huge threat, and volunteer clubs were deemed inadequate. Fire insurance firms and businesses drove the professionalization of fire forces. There was also a push to use fire-resistant building materials.

The threat of disease was ominous. Death rates were soaring. Summertime was especially hard. In June 1880, the *New York Times* reported that 1,297 people died in one week, two-thirds under the age of five, from a heatwave: "Undertaker wagons are busy on the East Side, the coffin maker's hammer has no rest." The prevalence of horses exacerbated the situation. In 1880, New York City had over one hundred thousand horses

In 1905, the New York City government was controlled by the Democratic Party and its
political machine known as Tammany Hall. In January, Superintendent of Buildings Isaac
A. Hopper, issued an order requiring that a special type of safety clutch be installed on all
New York City elevators. The order would have produced a huge windfall for the company.
Library of Congress, Prints and Photographs Division.

dropping sixty gallons of urine every day. Officials decried the "manure crisis." Overcrowded living conditions spread disease as well. In 1865, two-thirds of New Yorkers lived in tenements—350,000 per square mile, a level unmatched to that point. The influx of immigrants in the ensuing decades would exacerbate this housing crisis.

Corrupt political machines also hindered progress. New York City's budget expanded fifty-three-fold from 1830 to 1890. This increase helped mitigate urban problems but also led to the rise of political machines, "organizations are urban centers that mobilized the working class and established illicit relationships with business." Financial kickbacks were common. Some of these were diverted to supporters who, in turn, voted for the politicians. They also intimidated voters and let them know they were being watched.

Reformers were generally outraged. Robert Ingersoll said, "Tammany Hall bears the same relation to the penitentiary that the Sunday School does to the Church." But in time, the political machines would come under intense scrutiny from reformers.

WORKING-CLASS CULTURE IN THE GILDED AGE

Despite the huge difference in lifestyles and incomes, poor and rich households shared interests. For instance, some young laboring women looked on with curiosity and awe for the latest fashions more well-to-do women would wear. Some spent their accumulated pennies on ornate clothing to match or outdo the elite ladies.

In the late 1800s in New York City, an observer wrote:

> *If my lady wears a velvet gown, put together for her in an East Side sweatshop, may not the girl whose fingers fashioned it rejoice her soul by astonishing Grand Street with a copy of it next Sunday? My lady's in velvet and the East Side girl's is the cheapest, but it's the style that counts. In this land of equality, shall not one wear what the other wears? Does Broadway wear a feather? Grand Street wears two. Are trailing skirts seen on Fifth Avenue? Grand Street trails its yards with a dignity all its own.*[7]

Workers were also known for their rowdy behavior in theaters and in saloons. The bar served an essential function in working-class life for comradeship. It was the place where "workers dropped the discipline of the workplace and loosened self-control."[8] Brothels were also prevalent

The million-dollar corner on Thirty-Fourth Street and Broadway. In 1911, parts of the city were transforming rapidly with real estate prices appreciating. *George Bain Collection. Library of Congress, Prints and Photographs Division.*

in certain sections of working-class neighborhoods. According to *Intimacy Matters: A History of Sexuality in America*, most prostitutes were working-class women desperate for a living wage.

Saloons were for more than drinking. There was often an unspoken kinship—a man would buy a round of drinks for his friends, and they reciprocated. Coarse humor was shared while patrons played music or cards. Trade unions reinforced the comradery. It was a "we are in this together" mentality. That sensibility would be important for labor movements.

WHILE THE WORKING CLASS enjoyed such solidarity, there was also a darker side. Workers tended to divide each other by gender, class and race. Part of the reason was the swell of immigrants coming to New York's shores at this time. Most immigrants entered through New York's Castle Clinton, until the opening of Ellis Island in 1892. Many stayed in New York City and often made their home on the Lower East Side. Consequently, the once-tranquil neighborhood became the most crowded in the world. Immigrants hailed from Germany, Ireland, Russia, Italy, Greece and eastern European countries. Some were Jews fleeing Russian pogroms. Notably, very few came

Push carts sell clothes and other goods on crowded Lower East Side streets. *Wikimedia Commons.*

from China, due to the Chinese Exclusion Act passed in 1882, prohibiting the immigration of Chinese laborers.

Sadly, this ethnic diversity often divided workers. These divisions played out on the street and in the workplace. Skilled workers tended to look down on less-skilled workers. Trade unions tried to exclude Black people. The Irish, Polish and Italians fought for control over churches. Male workers often shut out female workers in their unions.

At the same time, there was unrest among the social elites. Divorces increased. Sons, in particular, had a difficult time following in their prominent fathers' footsteps. Progeny of the nation's richest men tended to be dissatisfied. The grandson of Commodore Vanderbilt, for example, complained, "My life was never destined to be quite happy. It was laid out along lines which I could foresee almost from earliest childhood. It has left me with nothing to hope for, with nothing definite to see or strive for."[9]

Rockefeller and Carnegie Give Away Much of Their Wealth

Maybe arising from this discontent, the two wealthiest New Yorkers at the close of the nineteenth century, oil tycoon John Rockefeller and steel magnate Andrew Carnegie, decided to infuse meaning into their fortunes by actively giving much of them away. Rockefeller professed a disgust for overindulging in material wealth. His values were informed largely by his Protestant faith:

> *I know of nothing more despicable and pathetic than a man who devotes all the waking hours of the day to making money for money's sake. The novelty*

of being about to purchase anything one wants soon passes because what people most seek cannot be bought with money. As I study wealthy men, I can see but one way in which they can secure a real equivalent for money spent, and that is to cultivate a taste for giving where money may produce an effect which will be a lasting gratification.[10]

Rockefeller's nemesis, Andrew Carnegie, expressed a similar sentiment. His was informed less by Protestantism and more by his intellectual reasoning of justice in resource allocation. He called on his peers to give away a significant portion of their wealth as well. Few others did though. He opined in his autobiography, "The problem of our age is that proper administration of wealth, that the ties of brotherhood may still bind together the rich and poor in harmonious relationship."[11]

Carnegie also questioned the common practice of bequeathing all wealth to one's children. "The parent who leaves his son enormous wealth generally deadens the talents and energies of the son, and tempts him to lead a less useful and less worthy life than he otherwise would." Carnegie was also in favor of the inheritance or so-called death tax. In his estimation, with the threat of much of one's estate going to the government, the rich person was more likely to give it away to noteworthy causes in life.

In effect, Carnegie called on members of his class to follow his example: "The duty of the man of wealth is to set an example of modest, unostentatious living, shunning display or extravagance; to provide moderately for the legitimate wants of those dependent upon him; and after doing so, to consider all surplus revenues which come to him simply as trust funds. He must bring to his poorer brethren his superior wisdom, experience, and ability to administer, doing for them better than they could do for themselves."[12]

In other words, according to Carnegie, the rich need to use their wealth to help the poor. The subtext of Carnegie's words is that the rich are inherently more talented and sophisticated and that these traits should be used to the betterment of poorer classes.

Carnegie, like Rockefeller, followed his preaching with action. Indeed, he donated almost 90 percent of his fortune before his death in 1919. The two asked others to follow suit. Few wealthy New Yorkers did. Most intended to leave their entire fortunes to their children.

In western New York, pioneer of modern-day photography George Eastman had founded his namesake company, Eastman Kodak. He began the company by patenting the first film in roll and by perfecting the Kodak Black camera. In the 1890s, his firm became the leading supplier of film stock

Eastman Kodak main office and factory in Rochester, New York, around 1900, near where George Eastman invented modern photography. Photography was growing in popularity and in ease of use during the Progressive Era. *Library of Congress, Prints and Photographs Division.*

internationally. Worth about $85 million (or $1.5 billion in present dollars), like Carnegie and Rockefeller, he was a noted philanthropist. In his town of Rochester, New York, he sponsored the Eastman School of Music, schools at the University of Rochester and parts of Rochester Institute of Technology. He also donated substantially to historically Black universities in the South.

As a result of Eastman's and other industrialist contributions, Rochester's cultural offerings multiplied. The city became known for excellence in music among upstate and western cities, largely from the Eastman School of Music. Opera houses and vaudeville theaters also sprang up in the western New York area beside Lake Ontario.

In this way, the two robber barons and Eastman were revolutionaries in their own class. By funding hospitals, libraries, schools, universities, parks, concert halls and more, they were greatly impacting society. Beyond their donations, though, they were challenging the status quo of their class. They might have had an inkling that something was changing in society. No longer were the working classes content with the social structure. Dissent was in the air.

Downtown Rochester, New York, around 1903. The picture shows the increased interest in leisure activities, such as the opera house and daily Vaudeville performances. *Library of Congress, Prints and Photographs Division.*

They were, in a sense, alerting their rich peers. But it was a call that went largely unheeded. An entirely new class was emerging. It would fill that gap between the working class and the rich. It was a class that would change the values, leisure and social construct of late nineteenth-century New York State.

2

Emergence of the Middle Class

In the final decades of the nineteenth century, the newly emerging middle class was gaining prominence. Workers in the middle class tended to comprise professions like small business owners, salespeople, managers and salaried organization men. It was a class that would change the values, leisure and social conditions of late nineteenth-century New York.

The middle class became a distinct social identity that imposed new values. This group saw itself as moral, righteous and frugal versus the working class, who they saw as frittering away their meager wages. The middle class also saw the upper class as overindulgent and squandering of big resources.

In many ways, the middle class was the "winner" of the Industrial Revolution. While many workers suffered, it did create new jobs in New York State, many of which were white-collar, like accountants, secretaries, office workers and clerks. These middle-class jobs carried more prestige and offered more benefits. In reality, the wages were not overall that much greater than some factory or mining work. Nor was a lot of the work more interesting. But middle-class workers prized themselves on not having to do physical labor.

Middle-class values expounded the virtues of the home. The sphere of domesticity was of paramount importance for women as mothers and wives. Freed from laborious chores with technological advancement, women could spend more time with children and on social activities. Men and women were considered to operate in different spheres. For men, it was outside the home in the workplace as the "hunter." For women, the sphere was in

Milk inspection station at a grocery on Manhattan's East Side, illustrating the greater emphasis on hygiene and health. *Collection of Maggie Land Blanck.*

the home and more as the "gatherer." In many homes were pianos where players would practice the notes from popular sheet music. Often the most expensive item in the home, the piano came to symbolize the tranquility and leisure of the middle class.[13]

Importantly, social class was—and still is—marked by more than simply income. It was delineated by values, attitudes and presentation. Along these lines, personal hygiene became important for the middle class. As examples, production and sales of toothpaste (or tooth polish) and deodorant rose in the latter decades of the nineteenth century. Milk, which had caused many diseases, was inspected more rigorously to ensure its purity and pasteurization. Milk inspection stations were set up around New York State.

EDUCATION IN UNIVERSITIES AND THROUGH CLUBS

With the increased access to capital and leisure time, the newly emerging middle class began an ambitious program to improve social conditions and educational opportunities. Some middle-class women enjoyed new opportunities to attend university. Academies welcoming them proliferated in the late nineteenth century: Smith in Northampton, Massachusetts, was founded in 1872; Wellesley in 1875; and Bryn Mawr in 1886. Moreover, several all-male institutions opened their doors—at least partway—to female students.

Women attending universities were met with mixed reactions. One student recalled, "In those benighted days, it was not socially the thing for a girl to go to college, and to go to Bryn Mawr College, which was regarded as extremely highbrow, was to damn oneself in the eyes of all right-thinking young males."[14]

Despite any misgivings, universities generally expanded the thinking of their students. As a result, some students began to question the status quo. For better or for worse, they were weakening the grip of Victorian ideals. Indeed, middle-class women were seeking new opportunities outside the traditional home setting.

With more young women graduating from college, other middle-class women pursued informal education through clubs and associations. These organizations would often cater to middle-aged women. The first was Sorosis, which was founded in New York City in 1868 by author and journalist Jane Croly, children's author Josephine Pollard and popular newspaper columnist Fanny Fern. This first-of-its-kind professional women's association was created because women were often excluded from membership in other organizations. As several founders were journalists, they were enraged about the New York Press Club excluding them.

The founders considered Sorosis's mission to promote "municipal housekeeping": applying to municipal problems the same principles of housekeeping that a well-educated woman was expected in the late nineteenth century to practice. The founders also hoped that the club would inspire confidence in women, and bring "womanly self-respect and self-knowledge."[15]

The club derived its name *Sorosis* from the botanical name for a fruit formed in the ovaries or receptacles of many flowers. It conveyed the idea of aggregation. The idea was to bring together or aggregate women in leading fields to learn from each other. Notable members included poet Elizabeth Allen and journalist Emily Roebling, wife of the famed Brooklyn Bridge engineer.

Yet this notion of aggregating women had limits. Some wanted the group to be more accommodating to women wage earners. Croly resisted, preferring to solve "our" problems and focusing on the self-growth of members.[16]

While Sorosis catered to women of a certain rank, it inspired a larger circle of middle-class women to pursue learning in art, literature and public issues in areas outside of New York City. Shortly after Sorosis was founded, Boston-based suffragettes started the New England Woman's Club.

Founded in Boston in 1868 by suffragettes Harriet Robinson and Caroline Severance, the New England Woman's Club met in the rear of the popular hotel Tremont House. Tremont House is probably best known for being among the first hotels in the nation to offer indoor plumbing and running water. By 1893, the club counted about 350 members. Despite its name, men joined too. Ralph Waldo Emerson was probably the most famous. The club's mission was to "provide a suitable place of meeting in Boston for the convenience of its members, and to promote social enjoyment and general improvement." Notable features included Monday teas and a horticulture club. Members heard different points of view on a variety of topics from lecturers, including Oliver Wendell Holmes and Ralph Emerson.[17]

Although founded independently, the emergence of the two organizations showcased the changing times. Middle-class women were becoming "more independent, involved in professionals, active in reform groups, and interested in self-development."[18]

Other clubs for women opened, too, including the Saturday Morning Club, the Brains Club and the Young Ladies Club. These were aimed at "general improvement" and the promotion of art, literature, education and public affairs.

In thriving western New York, the Chautauqua movement, named for nearby Lake Chautauqua, brought informal educational opportunities primarily to women in the fields of natural and social sciences, literature and languages.

With this initial success, the women's club movement soon multiplied and spawned national affiliations. Delegates from more than sixty women's clubs were brought together by Sorosis to form the General Federation of Women's Clubs, which had a mission of helping local clubs get better organized and encouraging clubs to work together on lobbying efforts for social reforms such as health, education, conservation and government reforms. Middle-class women were being exposed to new ideas.

Many of these middle-class women did not see reform as separate from their domestic duties. In their view, the better they could manage their homes and families, the better they could effectively make changes in their external environment. Michael McGerr's *A Fierce Discontent* illustrates this notion: "Organizations created in the struggle to change domesticity substantially increased the middle class's organizational strength. As activist women moved from conventional domesticity to the front lines of the middle-class public struggle, they brought a useful ideological weapon—ironically, couched in the rhetoric of domesticity itself. Swathing aggressive intentions in the reassuring warmth of home and hearth, this rhetorical device would become a key means of advancing the middle-class agenda in the new century."[19]

As an example, Frances Willard, a New York City–based educator and women's suffragist, wanted to "make the whole world homelike." Domestic science became a vehicle for change. Catherine Beecher, sister of the famed Harriet Beecher Stowe, was a strong proponent of women's education and suffrage. In contrast to contemporary views, Beecher believed women should not gain equality by competing with men but that "family was most important and homemaking was the profession women should be seeking."

HOME ECONOMICS AS A SCIENCE

Catherine Beecher made an early attempt to make home economics a science. Influenced by her sister, Catherine Beecher envisioned a "home economics course where women would receive an education in domestic chemistry, housing, and economical arrangement of storage in the home. She believed home economics to be a science and created the *Beecher Plan* for educating women in professions that were open to women: teaching, childcare, nursing, and conservation of the domestic state."[20] Though today middle and high school students often view home economics courses as trivial and overly domestic, the field was very important in its day in establishing a "scientific basis" for an improved home, family and society.

Later on, home economics as a movement caught fire with the 1891 book *The Chemistry of Cooking and Cleaning: A Manual for Housekeepers*, from chemist Ellen Richards. An expert in water quality, she applied scientific principles to the home. Her book—which was more of a guide—transformed how women conceptualized caring for their home. They thought about efficient ways to perform a domestic task in a more scientific manner. The underlying notion of Beecher's and others' home economics was that if homes were cleaner and family affairs more organized, these gains would translate to a better-functioning outside world. To improve society, one must first start with one's home and family.

The public caught on. Clubs for home economics started sprouting. The first official club meeting of home economics was held at the Lake Placid Club in upstate New York in 1899. The group showcased scientific principles in improving the home and encouraged attendees to "manage their own homes and be prepared for careers focused on people and the

An advanced cookery class for students in the Department of Domestic Science at the Mechanics Institute at Rochester, New York, class of 1909. *Courtesy of Rare & Manuscript Collections, Cornell University Library.*

environments around them." The club set out to put into practice the philosophy of home economics.

The media took little notice of the budding home economics movement. Within a decade though, the group created a national organization called the American Home Economics Association. In keeping with the scientific approach, the group created the *Journal of Home Economics*, first published in 1909.

Richards and Beecher both received recognition for advancing women's education and for applying scientific research into domestic situations. By 1914, home economics became more integrated with federal programs. The Smith-Lever Act of 1914 enacted a system of cooperative extension services connected to the Land Grant University System to "inform the people about current developments in agriculture, home economics, and other related issues."[21]

CHAUTAUQUA LECTURES

During this time, another adult education movement was sweeping the middle class of New York and around the United States. It influenced not only urban dwellers but also rural communities. Founded in rustic southwestern New York State and named for the nearby lake, Chautauqua was a series of lectures and entertainment for a community. It became known as the Chautauqua Institution. The organization was itinerant. Similar to a circus, the Circuit Chautauquas would pitch tents near towns and deliver lectures. By the mid-1920s, when Circuit Chautauquas were at their peak, they appeared in over ten thousand communities to audiences of more than forty-five million.

Speakers talked about prisons, social problems, worker exploitation, temperance, women's suffrage and child labor laws. Jane Addams, the founder of Hull House, was a famous speaker. These lectures opened the eyes of attentive audience members, many of whom had not been exposed to these issues.

Audiences were exposed to different types of music in the programming too. Many White audiences had only seen Black performers in minstrel shows. That, of course, was an exaggerated, stereotypical and often very mocking portrayal. In the Chautauqua program, they appreciated seeing Black singers perform gospel, rag and early jazz music, among other genres. Many saw opera vignettes for the first time too.

The series had a strong Christian undertone. Nondenominational Christian instruction, preaching and worship was part of the program. Both programmers and attendees saw both secular and spiritual knowledge as emanating from God and, therefore, vitally important. In later decades, though, the movement tried to become more mainstream to gain more money and followers. As a result, it lost credibility.

Still, its impact was strong. It exposed new ideas to different kinds of people. These ideas would take hold in reforms that were to come in the ensuing decades.

Michael McGerr, in *A Fierce Discontent*, explains the impact of the new middle class on overall society: "By the end of the nineteenth century, the middle class was giving distinctive new answers to the questions that confronted all social groups about the relationship between the individual and society, the nature of men, women, and the home, and the place of work and pleasure in daily life. These answers added up to a novel set of guiding values, a new ideology for the middle class. Victorianism gave way to progressivism. This ideological transformation not only drove middle-class people to change themselves and to make new homes; it also demanded that they change the world around them."[22]

THE SUPERRICH IN NEW YORK

While the middle class was forging its new identity, many of the superrich were spending their fortunes more garishly than previous generations on what was called conspicuous consumption. These families of the Gilded Age, the "new wealth," often had more money than previous generations, or "old money." But the old money families did not always accept the new families. What many craved was to be seen as cultured and educated, not just materially wealthy.

The changes in New York City's opulent apartments' appearance symbolized the increasing emphasis on materialism. During the 1830s in New York City, the wealthy built opulent apartments around Gramercy Park. The houses were plain and unornamented. This architecture stands in contrast to the ultra-gaudy mansions on Fifth Avenue from the later Gilded Age decades. By this time, the superrich embraced conspicuous consumption.

By the 1880s, Fifth Avenue was known as millionaire's row. "There is many a palace in Europe that would hide its diminished roof beside the sheer luxury of Fifth Avenue homes," claimed the popular monthly *Munsey's Magazine*.

One shining illustration of this consumption in 1883 was Vanderbilt hosting one of the most extravagant balls ever held in the city. Vanderbilt spent about $6 million in present money on the ball. New Yorkers watched guests arrive in full costumes. The press covered it well. This event allowed Mrs. Vanderbilt to catapult to higher societies by impressing the famed Mrs. Astor, who decided who was in and out of high society. Mrs. Astor was the social arbiter.

The Astors ruled the elite social scene. Throwing a lavish ball was a way to maintain standing. Some balls were so extravagant that observers compared them to the "splendor of Versailles in New York so grand that even King Louis likely had not witnessed a more dazzling sight." Resentment stirred at the glaring amounts of money spent. Newspapers condemned these over-the-top luxuries while most New York City residents were living in dire poverty.

But some of the elite circles claimed that these balls and similar displays of wealth were actually helping the economy and lower classes. They reasoned that they purchased many services and products, keeping storekeepers, merchants and manufacturers alive. It was clear that the gulf was not just in material goods but also in values of how money should be spent.

Some of the rich saw the dire conditions of the poor as a result of individual shortcomings rather than as a faulty economic system. Therefore, to improve the plight of the poor, one must work at an individual rather than a societal level. The notion was that anyone could rise out of poverty with enough effort.

Not all of the rich acted in this manner, of course. A case in point was Theodore Roosevelt, who grew up in a wealthy family. His outlook differed from those of his contemporaries. He believed in doing physical work and getting one's hands dirty. He reveled in his cowboy days in the Dakota Territory. He felt people should eschew a "slothful life" and preached the "doctrine of the strenuous life, the life of toil and effort, of labor and strife." He believed that through hard work and perseverance, one would develop his or her character.

Critics charged that much of this wealth was extracted from hardworking employees who barely received crumbs. They charged that the wealthy lived off the backs of exploited employees. This backlash would ultimately result in reforms to curb the excesses of the rich in favor of a more just society. The eventual passage of the income tax would serve as a prime example.

With their increased numbers and influence, social reformers increasingly defined a political, economic and social agenda that would mark the Progressive Era.

Part II

THE PROGRESSIVE ERA BEGINS

3

CALLS FOR REFORM

B y the 1880s and 1890s, social reformers began calling attention to the abject poverty often existing blocks from some of the wealthiest neighborhoods in the nation. Perhaps the most famous was reporter and writer Jacob Riis and his powerful photography.

JACOB RIIS—POWER OF PHOTOGRAPHY

An immigrant from Denmark, Riis arrived in the United States in 1870 with only forty dollars and a "locket containing a hair from a woman whom he loved." He worked several jobs, including bricklayer, ironworker and farmer. These jobs taught him about the struggles of laborers. Within three years, he landed a job as a police reporter. He covered stories of police involvement in the Lower East Side area. He saw a side of the city that few did. He had a keen interest in New York City's tenement life and the rough realities of its residents.

It is said that he used his camera to inspire profound change. His photos were of everyday residents' struggles, often showing them toiling under harsh labor conditions or crammed in a tenement. It was through this visual depiction in *How the Other Half Lives* that the public started to understand these sobering conditions. He "put those conditions on display in a package that was not to be ignored, and his career as a social reformer was launched."[23]

Riis's timing was lucky in that it was during this period that photography was advanced. These advances allowed Riis to capture for the public what had been impossible only a short while before. He started bringing his camera when he walked the neighborhood streets at night. He pioneered the technology to capture compelling day and night scenes. For night scenes, he was one of the earliest users of flash photography.

Before, the public had only read about these social struggles—if that—and now there was the visual accompaniment. His *How the Other Half Lives* captured the public's attention on this subject in a new way. Riis noted that his reason for portraying such a dark tableau was "that every man's experience ought to be worth something to the community from which he drew it, no matter what that experience may be."[24] Contemporary critics charge that Riis might have staged some of the scenes. Even if that is technically true, his photography still captured the essence of his subject—which to that point had all but been ignored.

The book touched not only the public but also politicians. Theodore Roosevelt, then a police commissioner and later the governor of New York and eventually the president of the United States, famously stated to the photographer, "I have read your book, and I have come to help." The two investigated the stark conditions of the neighborhood, which inspired Roosevelt to act for much of his political career. Riis went on to write other notable books in the same vein, including *Children of the Tenements* and *Out of Mulberry Street*.[25]

Riis's photography emphasized the ever-widening gap between the rich and poor, as well as the deteriorating housing conditions of immigrants. Images captivated the public in a way that words could not. Many New Yorkers had no idea of abject poverty. The book brought sympathy to groups that had been overlooked and even forgotten. From these books and others like it, some New Yorkers began to see the importance of individual members feeling responsible for their communities' well-being.

The Social Gospel

Some Protestant ministers also felt compelled to make significant social change. A cornerstone of Christianity was, after all, to help the poor and the disenfranchised. Accordingly, some ministers formed the movement of the social gospel. This undertaking became the religious wing of the budding progressive movement. The social gospel sought to apply Christian ethics and theology to societal ills, including economic inequality, alcoholism, racism, slums, labor exploitation, education gaps and child labor. At the heart of this gospel was the Lord's Prayer from the Book of Matthew: "Thy kingdom come, Thy will be done on earth as it is in heaven."

The Presbyterians described their social gospel goals by proclaiming, "The great ends of the church are the proclamation of the gospel for the salvation of humankind; the shelter, nurture, and spiritual fellowship of the children of God; the maintenance of divine worship; the preservation of truth; the promotion of social righteousness; and the exhibition of the Kingdom of Heaven to the world."[26]

Many Protestants were repelled by the rampant poverty and labor exploitation they saw around them. They wanted to integrate their religious texts and teachings with social change. The social gospel provided that. It was theologically based advocacy for intervention. Adherents pushed for mandatory schooling for the poor. Their rationale was that education would improve the students' skills and, more importantly, their morality. Social gospel followers also pushed hard to abolish childhood labor and shorten workdays for adults. They met with mixed success.

One of the most famous successes was the Young Men's Christian Association (YMCA). The YMCA was created to aid rural young people in coping with the city without losing their religion. The YMCA stated its mission as helping its members develop a healthy "mind, body, and spirit." In the 1890s, it became a powerful instrument in the social gospel by providing humanitarian work, charitable activities and athletic facilities. Donors supported these organizations to "give youth an outlet and discourage the temptations of alcohol, gambling, and prostitution."

The social gospel spawned centers throughout the United States. In the South, mostly led by Baptists, it emphasized obliterating what they saw as personal vices: alcohol, public swearing, gambling and illegal corruption.

In New York State, the most well-known social gospel Baptist pastor was Walter Rauschenbusch. Years after studying at the Rochester Theological Seminary in Rochester, New York, he led a congregation in Manhattan's notorious Hell's Kitchen. At the turn of the twentieth century, the area was home to dockworkers and was a bastion of poor Irish and Italian immigrants. Rauschenbusch preached against the "selfishness of capitalism" and promoted a form of Christian socialism that supported the creation of labor unions and cooperative economics."[27]

The social gospel movement was never a unified front. There were differing opinions about the role of the church and whether or not to embrace

Walter Rauschenbusch sought to make the social gospel movement part of Christianity. He noted a mutually dependent relationship between theology and social reform. He stated that the social gospel movement needed a "theology to make it effective and likewise, theology needs the social gospel to vitalize it."*

This notion underscored his key work, *A Theology for the Social Gospel*. In this controversial publication, Rauschenbusch asserts that the "individualistic gospel has made sinfulness of the individual clear, but it has not shed light on institutionalized sinfulness. It has not evoked faith in the will and power of God to redeem the permanent institutions of human society from their inherited guilt of oppression and extortion." He felt that Christianity had strayed too far from its original intent. He encouraged a return to the "Kingdom of God" for "prophetic, future-focused ideology and a revolutionary, social and political force that understands all creation to be sacred." For Rauschenbusch, that is what would combat long-term what he saw as the sinful social order.

Though not embraced at the time, his shedding of light on institutionalized sinfulness informed the thinking of prominent civil rights leaders over a half-century later.

---

* Walter Rauschenbusch, *Theology for the Social Gospel* (New York: Macmillan, 1917).

any socialistic ideologies. As a result of this lack of unity, the social gospel never really caught on among lay churchgoers. It remained a movement largely among liberal pastors. Some pastors and laypeople believed the social reforms were distracting from their more important role of spreading the eternal lifesaving message of the Gospel. Though the movement itself lasted only a few decades, with its breakdown after World War I, it has had a lasting impact. Historians link the social gospel to the eventual passage of both the women's suffrage amendment and to Prohibition. The social gospel movement has been described as the "most distinctive American contribution to world Christianity." Echoes of it were in famed civil rights movement speeches in the 1960s, including those of Reverend Martin Luther King Jr.

The Progressive Era Begins

> *Nothing so needs reforming as other people's habits. Fanatics will never learn that, though it is written in letters of gold across the sky.*
> —Mark Twain

REFORMERS' AGENDA

While the social gospel operated through a Christian lens, the progressive reformers in New York had more secular aims. They sought to remold what they saw as personal vices by banning liquor, abolishing prostitution and discouraging divorce. All too aware of poor labor conditions, they fought to improve the lives of employees with shorter workweeks and more safety regulations. They also sought to protect children from labor exploitation. In the rural parts of New York State, they also aimed to modernize the agrarian way of life.

In total, these reforms were an audacious attempt to "remake Americans" to new ways of conduct. This transformation, they knew, would have to be across social classes to bring long-lasting change. They wanted to change institutions like large corporations—and the businessmen as well. Their efforts were not only in changing institutions but also the people behind them. One of their first would be in changing public perceptions about the poor. Another would be improving the crowded and unsanitary housing conditions for many New York residents.

4

ERADICATING POVERTY
AND HOUSING REFORMS

T he prevailing notion was that the poor were responsible for their plight. Many assumed impoverished people were lazy. Reformers sought to change not only the physical conditions of the poor but also the stereotypes and misconceptions about them. They understood that the overwhelming demands of the urban and rural poor were so great that outsiders needed to step in to improve their situations. Religious institutions played a key role in combatting poverty.

CHURCH-BASED PROGRAMS

In New York, churches formed anti-poverty programs. The more traditional church-sponsored revival urban outreach programs and city missions did not prove successful. Some of the poor were reluctant to be preached to. Moreover, these mission programs addressed symptoms, like providing for the hungry and homeless, but they did not solve the causes. However, two organizations spawned from church-based programs made a lot of traction: the YMCA and the Salvation Army.

A reason for the success of the Salvation Army was its on-the-street approach to social action. A Methodist minister, William Booth, and his wife began the organization in East London, England, in 1865. The couple wanted to decrease London's poverty. Their approach was far more active and innovative than what most churches were willing to do.

They offered a network of soup kitchens, a secondhand thrift store and many social services.

In 1880, George Railton and Emma Westbrook, along with six female "soldiers," brought the Salvation Army to New York City. In 1891, the Salvation Army opened its first men's food and shelter depot in Greenwich Village and a comparable shelter for women. Soon after, it opened a facility to serve food and provide safe lodging on the notorious Bowery. The Army offered a plethora of social service programs, outreach programs, soup kitchens, food pantries, foster care organizations, resident programs for the developmentally disabled and employment training centers. The organization was mission-centered. It sought to "bring the Gospel of Jesus Christ to the downtrodden and lost among us."

Also started in England and transported to New York was the Young Men's Christian Association (YMCA). Founded in 1844 by George Williams in London, the group aimed to "put Christian principles into practice by developing a healthy mind, spirit, and body." It emphasized youth activities like sports, Christian teaching and humanitarian community service. In later decades, reacting to industrialization and urban poverty, the group provided "low-cost housing in a safe Christian environment for rural young men and women journeying to the cities." The YMCA preached in the streets and, like the Salvation Army, combined social ministry with religious thought and action.

In 1896, the West Side YMCA opened on the then remote West Fifty-Seventh Street at Eighth Avenue on a site that railroad magnates Cornelius Vanderbilt and his son William bought for $165,000. The location was so far uptown that few thought it could attract members. Despite its out-of-the-way location, the venue became the first YMCA to offer a dormitory. YMCA officials added a three-hundred-bed residence in 1912.

In addition to the Salvation Army and YMCA, Protestant reform-minded ministers began the Institutional Church movement in New York City in the 1890s. These ministers sought to recapture support the church had lost in the city among the laboring poor. William Muhlenberg and Thomas Beecher pioneered this movement. Their idea was to use church buildings for more than prayer a few times per week. At St. George's Episcopal Church in New York, they used the church building each day for game rooms, employment services, food and clothing distribution centers, sewing and cooking classes, clinics and hospitals.

HOUSING REFORMS

For secular social reformers, helping the poor was not just providing resources but also changing laws to improve living conditions. This was a central tenet of the Progressive Era—to transform society, one must start with individuals and their home lives. In New York, many residents were living in desperate poverty in unsanitary and extremely crowded conditions. In the late nineteenth century, few tenements had indoor plumbing or toilets.

As immigrants flowed into New York City, the new arrivals faced dark, cramped living conditions in tenement housing that dominated neighborhoods like the Lower East Side. Greedy landlords turned once single-family homes into multi-family housing with very poor conditions and years of neglect. To pack in as many tenants as possible, landlords erected walls to make more apartments and cut corners on all the materials. Most apartments had no running water, toilets or ventilation. Diseases spread easily. Poor immigrants with little money and no command of English or the city took what they could get. By 1900, "more than 80,000 tenements had been built and housed 2.3 million people, two-thirds of the total city population."[28]

In Jacob Riis's ground-breaking book *How the Other Half Lives*, referenced previously, he commented on how neighborhood children rarely got to partake in nearby activities. "Out of forty-eight boys twenty had never seen the Brooklyn Bridge that was scarcely five minutes' walk away, three only had been in Central Park, fifteen had known the joy of a ride in a horse-car. The street, with its ash-barrels and its dirt, the river that runs foul with mud, are their domain."

Most residents in neighborhoods Riis described lived in very cramped tenements. Riis advocated for badly needed improvements to the safety, hygiene and privacy of tenements.

The Greenwich Village Society for Historic Preservation describes the formation of tenements:

> *The typical pre-law tenement was about four stories tall and housed ten to twenty families on a narrow twenty-five-foot-wide lot. There were generally four units on each of the upper floors, with a pair of stores and two rear apartments on the first floor. Each apartment had two or three rooms. Windows only lit one room in each apartment; thus, most rooms had no immediate access to natural light or fresh air. These apartments were not supplied with gas or water, although both gas lines and water*

lines had already been laid on Village streets. Some tenements had a single water line with a tap in the hall on each floor. Most, however, had both the water source and toilets in the shallow backyard. In some cases, the toilets were placed between a front building and a rear tenement erected at the back of the lot.[29]

To improve these conditions, relief workers persuaded then-governor Theodore Roosevelt to support the Tenement House Commission to formally study the housing issue. In February 1901, the commission concluded that new legislation was needed. Consequently, the New York State Legislature held hearings, and in two months, the Tenement Housing Act of 1901 was signed into law. Reformers pressured the New York State Legislature to establish a housing standard: light, ventilation and sanitation. Other cities followed New York's example.

HISTORY OF HOUSING REFORM

Housing reform began in 1879 to answer concerns about dire housing conditions. The law had many loopholes and was not successful, "however, the law succeeded in prohibiting the construction of buildings with windowless interior rooms, requiring that all rooms have windows facing the street, rear yard, or an interior shaft. The most common design resulting from this requirement was the 'dumbbell,' so named because the required air shafts created a building footprint that resembled the shape of a dumbbell weight."[30]

In reality, though, the shafts that the 1879 law mandated provided almost no light or air to apartments. The problem often got worse, as residents began throwing their garbage out of their windows and into these shafts. Shaft windows also decreased privacy. But for landlords, it was a windfall. Some estimates put their return on investment at 20 percent. They had no incentive to improve their properties.

Reformers had fought hard for livable conditions. By the turn of the twentieth century, they made marked progress. Following the recommendations of a commission, the New York State Legislature passed the new Tenement House Act of 1901. This banned dark, unventilated tenement buildings in the state. It tried to close the loopholes in the two previous acts, ensuring the air shafts and courtyard were designed for garbage removal.

The law created disincentives to construct twenty-five-foot-wide lots. Consequently, after this law, landlords built tenements on wider lots. Importantly, these new tenements had more light coming in, windows in each room and an indoor toilet for every two families. Landlords preferred building these new tenements on corners so they could more economically meet the law's requirements. They also tended to be taller—above four stories—to receive more revenue. Developers rushed to build tenements in 1901, just before the new law went into effect.

The new 1901 law did not go unchallenged. Landlords asserted in a court case that the law violated the Fourteenth Amendment of the Constitution, which provided for citizenship rights and equal protection under the law. In the *Tenement House Department of the City of New York v. The Owners*, the jury sided with the city. A similar case was the *Tenement House Department v. Katie Moeschen*, an owner fighting changes. Owners first challenged the verdict in U.S. appellate court and then with the U.S. Supreme Court in 1906.

Appellate courts would not reverse the decision. The tenement owners had run out of options. They were going to have to relent and provide basic amenities, like proper ventilation systems, indoor toilets and fire safeguards.

What brought about these reforms? For decades before, the belief was that philanthropists, wealthy individuals or private organizations would cure poor housing and other maladies. During the Progressive Era, though, there was a shift from seeing private citizens as the answer to viewing the government and power of the courts as part of reform. The progressive belief was also that cleaner cities meant better citizens. There was a fear of diseases like smallpox and tuberculosis. Thus the public saw self-preservation and self-interest in trying to improve housing conditions.

To compensate for poor housing conditions, reformers advocated for public parks, baths, gymnasiums, swimming pools and auditoriums. Again, they stressed the link between clean citizens and a better society. A New York State commission declared that bathhouses had a "favorable effect upon character. Parks promoted desirable types of humanity."

Reformers' efforts did not stop in the city. In rural New York State and in farms across the nation, they launched the country life movement. Paradoxically, the chief proponents were from the city. Many were urban, middle-class activists, state and federal agricultural officials and academics from universities like Cornell in Ithaca, New York. They assessed that farmers were isolated, and a lack of cooperation was hindering rural life and farming efficiencies. One observer noted, "Perhaps the one great underlying social difficulty among American farmers is their comparatively isolated mode of life. Rural life is real evil. Present-day living is so distinctively social, and progress is so dependent upon social agencies, social development is so rapid, that if the farmer is to keep his status, he must be fully in step with the rest of the army. He must secure the social viewpoint."[31]

5

CHILD LABOR LAWS

Child labor was also a major platform item. Much of the public had little idea of how pervasive it was. One visitor to a southern textile mill around 1900 described an incident:

> *Walking up the long, orderly building, deafened by the racket, you become suddenly aware of a little gray shadow flitting restlessly up and down the aisles—a small girl, and with bare feet and pale face. She has a worn and anxious aspect as if a weight of care and responsibility rested already on her baby shoulders....A thread breaks first at one end of the long frame then at the other. The tiny fingers repair the damage at the first place and she walks listlessly to the other. With a great shock, it dawns on you that this child is working.*[32]

Jacob Riis saw a lot of child exploitation while reporting on the Lower East Side as a police reporter. He wrote, "Wherever child labor exists, wherever the home is oppressed, wherever the street is the only playground of the children, wherever they are dragged into the police courts when they ought to be in school, there is the slum waiting to raise its head."

Reformers sought drastic child labor laws. Employers resisted the laws. So did families who depended on the income. They identified three major obstacles to progress for advancing children's rights. First, employers saw children as instruments of their profit. They had no incentive to make changes. Second, much of the public believed poverty was a necessary and expected human condition. They did not see a real reason to change it.

Children making flowers in a tenement in the Lower East Side of New York City. Child labor exploitation was rampant. *Courtesy of the Jacob Riis Collection at the Museum of the City of New York and the Visiting Nurse Service of New York Record Archives & Special Collections, Columbia University.*

Many doubted whether a change would even be possible. Third, officials charged with enforcing the law were often corrupt and easily paid off.[33]

After years, reforms were won. A compulsory education law stated that children had to attend school until they reached the age of fourteen. For ages fourteen to sixteen, they had to obtain working papers. In reality, many lied about their ages, and parents often went along. General society was unsympathetic to this plight. Many believed that the government should not dictate at what age someone could be allowed to start working. If one wanted to work at a younger age, then he or she should be allowed. But this belief system was based on a blind faith that wages were fair and that conditions were humane. It also did not account for families pressuring a child who might not want to work.

Under the new laws, children had to prove by birth certificate that they were the age they claimed. Further, they had to pass a simple test in English and arithmetic and present proof of at least 130 days of school attendance.

Children rolling cigars in a tenement in the Lower East Side of New York City. Many dropped out of school to earn a meager income for their families. *Courtesy of the Jacob Riis Collection at the Museum of the City of New York and the Visiting Nurse Service of New York Record Archives & Special Collections, Columbia University.*

They also had to be declared physically fit for work by a medical officer. These laws were meant to discourage parents from easily offering up their children to work for meager wages. Yet many tried to evade the system.[34]

CHILDREN'S BUREAU

In the early twentieth century, reformers trying to curb child labor exploitation pushed for a federal agency focused on protecting minors. Florence Kelley, a social activist and community nurse, thought of the idea while reading a newspaper article on a pest that was destroying cotton crops in the South. The U.S. Department of Agriculture was dispatching teams of scientists to investigate.

She noted that the government responded rapidly to solve the cotton pest problem. When it came to protecting children, the government dragged its feet. She and other nurses decided that a children's bureau in the federal government was needed for their cause to be taken seriously. They envisioned a bureau to lobby and pass laws in favor of children.

She conferred with the founder of the Visiting Nurse Service Henry Street Settlement, Lillian Wald. Leveraging her substantial political connections, Wald arranged to see President Teddy Roosevelt in the White House, outlining the argument for a national bureau for children. The president agreed, seeing the program's merits. He introduced a bill to Congress. But Congress had no interest in conducting hearings on the matter.

Kelley traveled to Washington, D.C., and pleaded her case. "If money is being spent for the eradication of scabies in cattle, why not spend a small portion of these amounts to save ¼ of our blind from being blind, to make the deaf hear and to give to those charged with the care of the wards of the nation, a bureau of central information?"[35]

Changes took time. A year after her trip to D.C., she served on a committee of the Second Conference on Charities and Corrections, which required children's attendance at school regardless of their income. In other words, poor families could not claim financial hardship as a reason for keeping their kids out of school. The bill provided aid to families where needed so that their children could attend school. But to reform advocates, it wasn't enough. A Federal Children's Bureau was needed.

Then, in April 1912, it finally happened. President Taft signed into law the bill that Wald and Kelley had advocated for seven years before. The government was to fund the Federal Children's Bureau. Kelley proclaimed her vision for it as a "great center that would draw from all corners of the earth the latest information on child care, and educate teachers, parents and health officials on the best methods available. A new conception of the child—free of motion, up-looking, the ward of the nation."[36]

Indeed, improvements in children's care were numerous. Schools improved, childbirth deaths decreased and more family courts opened. The treatment of orphans and disabled children vastly improved. Importantly, legislation was passed to control the number of hours children could work. The problem was then the enforcement of these laws.

Ultimately, the organization was well-intentioned but carried limited power. It aggregated and disseminated information. But it lacked true enforcement power. Reformers knew that they could not rely solely on the government or law enforcement to make lasting changes. So, they sought innovative ways to improve the lives of New Yorkers and, ultimately, all Americans.

Part III

Improving Quality of Life

6

SETTLEMENT HOUSES

In the late nineteenth century, reformers enacted novel ideas for combatting poverty and improving education and health care. One such initiative—which lasts to the present day—was the settlement house. Settlement houses differed from other agencies in several essential ways. First, unlike many charitable organizations, they were not religious. In fact, many went out of their way to promote their secular worldview. Second, the caregivers did not just work but also resided at the settlement house. This arrangement brought a sense of community and sent a message to the neighborhood that they were not just serving it but were a part of it. Consequently, settlement house workers often forged deep bonds with their clients.

Perhaps the most crucial distinction was that settlement houses prided themselves on solving the underlying causes of the problems their clients faced, not just the symptoms. For example, a settlement house focused on improving health care would do far more than dispense prescriptions and bandages. It would teach residents how to improve their hygiene, self-care and food preparation to maintain sanitary conditions and avoid future illnesses. Settlement house workers also aimed to "treat the whole person," often offering classes in education and the arts. Settlement houses sprang up from frustration with bureaucracy and corrupt local politicians, as well as stodgy establishments like hospitals or asylums. Indeed, some settlement house workers emerged from these institutions, where they felt their feedback or suggestions would fall on deaf ears. They also wanted to treat their clients with more respect and empathy than was typically the case in those places.

They sought to "bring the rich and poor of society together in both physical proximity and social interconnectedness."

Many residents of poor neighborhoods avoided hospitals, as they often feared doctors. Few could pay for help anyway, as insurance was rare. Some families also encouraged—or mandated—their children quit school at a young age to work and contribute to the family income. Functioning as social workers, settlement house workers would discourage this practice and try to show families the long-term benefits of education.

Since settlement houses were residential, workers tended to be unmarried, middle-class, idealistic and unconventional young men and women. Generous and wealthy benefactors and philanthropists often funded them. Sometimes, clients paid a nominal amount for services rendered. Usually, there was no direct public funding, though some settlement houses sought private-public partnerships.

Early Settlement Houses

The first settlement house was in England with the founding of Toynbee Hall in Whitechapel in London's East End. It was an early model that emphasized service delivery, like providing shelter to poor neighborhood residents. Most of the staff were university students and faculty. The prevailing notion in both England and the United States at the time was that the poor were mostly responsible for their plight. Society tended to see the poor as lazy and lacking virtues. Settlement house leaders reversed that notion. They argued that most poverty came from industrialization, rampant income inequality, lack of worker protections, lack of education and an uneven playing field.

In the United States, the oldest settlement house was the University Settlement in New York City's Lower East Side, founded in 1886. It was located at 184 Eldridge Street, not far from the famed, ornate Eldridge Synagogue. The University Settlement still exists today, despite the rapid changes around it. Stanton Coit and Charles Stover founded it to provide courses for immigrants who were flooding the city, many of whom knew little English or had few marketable skills. Many also lacked basic hygiene to withstand the harsh urban conditions in the extremely crowded Lower East Side. The University Settlement provided a library, the first kindergarten in the United States and even the first public baths. Many of these features were brand new to arriving immigrants.

Initially, University Settlement workers were all male and recent college graduates. Many wore two hats—reformers delivering necessary services and writers influencing the culture through articles on social injustices. Residents of the settlement read like a Who's Who in journalism. They include Walter Weyl, a founding editor of the *New Republic*, and Howard Brubaker, who served as a columnist for the prestigious *New Yorker* shortly after its founding in 1925. Their writing helped spur a national conversation about the slum housing, precarious employment and deprived health care of their city's residents. The University Settlement paved the way for others.

The most notable alumni of the settlement workers were George and Ira Gershwin, who became famous composers and writers of groundbreaking musicals, including *An American in Paris* and *Porgy and Bess*. Other alumni include Jacob Javits and future mayor of New York City Abraham Beame. Before she became first lady, Eleanor Roosevelt volunteered there.

In Chicago, Jane Addams and Ellen Starr started Hull House in 1889 to provide educational and recreational resources for European immigrants. Hull House grew to thirteen buildings and offered cutting-edge educational and arts programming. It is noted as the standard-bearer for future settlement houses. The mirror to the University Settlement, staffed by men, Hull House was staffed primarily by university women. They offered classes in literature, history, home economics and home-based skills, like sewing. The club serviced both children and adults.

Hull House was a quintessentially Progressive Era undertaking. It served the needs of society from settlement workers who lived there. Also, its founders used data to make decisions and advocate for change. Addams reinforced this principle through her "three Rs" to summarize Hull House's mission: residence, research and reform. For the research portion, Hull House workers researched the neighborhood to study reasons behind poverty. They then leveraged these studies to arm Hull House residents to advocate for social change for the immigrant population. They lobbied on behalf of child labor reform, women's suffrage, health care reform and immigration status. Observers referred to the Hull House neighborhood as a "laboratory upon which the social and philanthropic groups of Hull House elitists had tested their theories and formulated their challenges to the establishment."[37]

Jane Addams was, in the final analysis, as much a reformer and innovator as a social services leader. She opened Chicago's first public playground, bathhouse and public gymnasium. She challenged politicians and academics to rethink some of the causes of crime. Having studied child behavior, she concluded that "children robbed of childhood were likely to become dull, sullen men and women working mindless jobs or criminals for whom the adventure of crime became the only way to break out of the bleakness of their lives."[38] Addams's work led to a juvenile court system and a playground association.

Hull House's advocacy efforts contributed to the passage of a slew of legislation during the Progressive Era and later, including child labor laws, occupational safety, compulsory education, workers' compensation and pension laws.

Hull House also became known in supernatural circles. Before Addams moved in, the house had a reputation for its haunted attic. According to observers, resident ghosts could have included the wife of Charles Hull, for whom the house is named, or those who died when the house was a home for the aged. Even Jane Addams thought the house might be ghostly. She is said to have privately mentioned that one of the second-floor bedrooms might be haunted. Addams allegedly witnessed a woman in white ghost there. Years later, a group of girls performing at the theater next door saw the same ghost.

Sadly, Hull House closed its doors in 2012 and filed for bankruptcy.

HENRY STREET SETTLEMENT

Perhaps the most famous settlement in New York City that thrives to the present day is the Henry Street Settlement. Its founder, Lillian Wald, did not set out to open a settlement house. She was a young nurse from Rochester, New York, who studied at New York Hospital. She grew disillusioned with the hospital bureaucracy and poor doctors' bedside manner.

Wald wrote in her autobiography, *House on Henry Street*, that she loved interacting with patients when she could. But the hospital management seemed to frown on it and seemed to her to be consumed with rigid restrictions. Everything had to be done precisely—when patients' temperatures were taken, when food was to be eaten and so on.

In one telling account, Lillian relayed to a doctor a light moment she shared with a patient. "I told Mr. Anderson, the patient, a funny story, and he laughed. Really laughed. I think you'll find him much more cheerful."

The doctor, though, was unamused. He stared at her with an annoyed expression. "Laughter is likely to be a strain on him just now. When humor is indicated, I shall prescribe it. Nurse, what is his temperature?"[39]

Often sensing they were a burden to medical staff, patients felt comfortable with Wald. One patient expressed this sentiment, stating, "She don't make you feel you've committed a crime by getting sick and needin' more help than you can pay for."[40]

From countless incidents like these, Wald questioned the health care system. After graduating from nursing school, she worked at a juvenile asylum. She recounts in her autobiography how the odds were stacked against the kids. In one incident, she brought one of the asylum residents to a dentist, as he was having a toothache. The dentist quickly noted that he would need to extract the tooth. "How would he know so quickly," she thought. He did not even examine the boy's mouth. She felt herself getting angry at this injustice. She could not keep silent.

She scolded the dentist for so hastily deciding to pull the boy's tooth without trying to save it. He could have lost his tooth unnecessarily. She threatened to take the boy to her own dentist. Then, the dentist relented. He agreed to examine the boy. He determined that he was able to save the tooth. Wald saw how the system gave no consideration for the individual.

Feeling overwhelmed by the system, Wald volunteered to teach a class in home care and hygiene for Jewish immigrant women. Most students spoke limited English and gave blank stares when Lillian spoke. After several lessons, Lillian got the hint and began speaking in simpler English. She taught them lessons on hygiene and good health. She felt empathy toward her students. She wanted to see each one as an individual. Her previous employers would often see them all in one way: "those poor" or "the disadvantaged." But she remembered a lesson she first learned in nursing school: what is needed is not pity but rather a practical solution.

Then one day while she was teaching, Lillian's life changed. While she was teaching her class, a weeping child sheepishly entered the room. Lillian looked up from her bed-making demonstration. A tense silence fell on the room.

"Your mother is sick. Is that it?" Lillian asked.[41]

The child nodded.

Sensing the urgency, Lillian dismissed the class and followed the child into the chaotic neighborhood over broken-down roads and foul-smelling uncovered garbage cans. Lillian had to hold the bundle of sheets against her nose as she went by. She had no idea what she was going to encounter.

She finally reached a dilapidated tenement, where she climbed up muddy steps in a dark hallway. The floors creaked. Odors defiled the hallways. Lillian could barely see anything ahead of her due to the poor lighting. She held tightly to the broken railing to keep her balance. The child stopped and opened a door. She finally entered a two-room apartment, where she found a young woman lying in bed in a dingy room. There was no heat and virtually no light.

The child pointed to her mother. Lillian saw a sick woman lying down in the distance. She hemorrhaged when she had given birth two days before. Dried blood covered her. A family of seven crowded in the two rooms in addition to those to whom they leased tiny amounts of space to pay rent.

Lillian was horrified. She had never seen anything like it. She would later call this incident "baptism by fire." She cared for the sick woman and the new baby. She reassured the anguished family. She cared for their medical needs and their hygiene needs. She placed fresh sheets on the soiled bed and scrubbed the hard-worn floors. She cooked them a simple meal. As she was leaving the tenement, she paused. She turned toward the frightened family and promised to return. They kissed her hand in gratitude.

This experience would mark a fundamental change for Lillian. She rethought her life's work. No longer did she see herself as "just a nurse" or a part of an institution. Nor was she content with merely teaching hygiene

Girls learning to sew at the Henry Street Settlement in the Lower East Side in New York City. *Courtesy of the Jacob Riis Collection at the Museum of the City of New York and the Visiting Nurse Service of New York Record Archives & Special Collections, Columbia University.*

A Henry Street Settlement nurse in New York City's Lower East Side crossing rooftops to avoid going up and down the treacherous stairs. *Courtesy of Visiting Nurse Service of New York, Record Archives & Special Collections, Columbia University.*

classes to immigrants. She wanted to care for the sick but also change the social conditions that led to abject poverty and unseemly conditions. Amid the poverty surrounding her, she found a way to use her studies. She had another realization: the public did not know about these horrid conditions. If they did, she reasoned, more would be done to alleviate suffering.[42]

With her classmate Mary Brewster, Wald set out to live among those she intended to serve in the Lower East Side. The two ventured out each day to tend to the medical needs of the community.

Eventually, their practice grew, and their financial backer, Jacob Schiff, bought them a house on Henry Street in 1893. That became the Henry Street Settlement and Visiting Nurse Service. The house is still the Henry Street Settlement as of this writing. Over the decades, the settlement hired more nurses. One of the most successful programs was the partnership with Metropolitan Life Insurance. With the company's agents, the settlement distributed a pamphlet called a *War on Consumption* in many different languages. It was a guide for fighting tuberculosis.

THOUGH THE HENRY STREET Settlement focused on providing health care services, settlement workers soon realized that to address their underlying neighborhood issues, they would need to broaden their outreach. The Henry Street Settlement pioneered the city's first playgrounds, school nurses, kindergartens and school lunches. In typical Progressive Era fashion, the leaders did so by convincing local and state politicians through test cases and data collection. For example, to persuade the Department of Education of the need for school nurses, Wald started with one school nurse and measured the impact on student attendance. The data showed the efficacy of school nurses.

The settlement also opened the Grand Street Playhouse across the street. By putting on artistic productions, the settlement was able to tap into the creativity of the immigrant population it served. That was a novelty for a group that had been seen mostly as cheap labor. The settlement also provided racially integrated classes in educational, artistic and job training.

In the dining room of the Henry Street Settlement, two breakthrough ideas emerged. The organization that would become the NAACP (National Association for the Advancement of Colored People) was conceived, as well as advocacy for the nation's first children's bureau, which protected children from exploitative labor practices.

Opposite: Reformers started free kindergarten to bolster early childhood education, particularly among lower-income populations. *Visiting Nurse Service of New York Records, Archives & Special Collections, Health Sciences Library, Columbia University.*

Above: Henry Street Settlement on NBC radio as the organization became more prominent. *Courtesy of Visiting Nurse Service of New York Record Archives & Special Collections, Health Science Library, Columbia University.*

The University and Henry Street Settlements are probably the most famous and well known today. But New York City had many other settlement houses as part of a national trend. "Settlement Houses grew in popularity with over 400 in 32 states by 1913. At its peak in 1920, there were almost 500 across the US. Soon after, the number declined."[43]

Perhaps the most long-lasting contribution of settlement houses was treating members of a community as individuals rather than as cogs to run through an anonymous education or health care system. At their best, settlement houses reshaped the way society viewed the poor. Settlements demonstrated how in the right settings, they could improve their situations. Settlement houses also catered to the whole individual, encouraging residents to express themselves artistically. They showed that serving the poor did not need to be religious in nature, as had been the case for much of the nineteenth century. Finally, they gave rise to academic fields that had previously been given little attention at universities. Education, nursing, public health and environmental studies took on new rigor as academic subjects and research, some of which stemmed from settlement house efforts. They also provided a safe place for leisure—a rarity for the lower classes of the early twentieth century.

LEISURE AND PLAY

PLAYGROUNDS

Reformers fought to have safe places for residents to enjoy leisure activities and for children to play. Many advocated the playground in response to the high traffic accidents and gangs on the streets. Lillian Wald, founder of the Henry Street Settlement in New York City's Lower East Side in 1891, was instrumental in developing the nation's first playgrounds.

Wald had witnessed children at their outdoor games dangerously dodging pushcarts and vehicles. Her solution was to open a playground by combining the Henry Street Settlement's backyard with adjacent ones. Her original plan was to use this space for "cripples, chronic invalids, and convalescents" but changed her mind after realizing the need for a safe place for children to play. The playground was an immediate hit in the neighborhood.

She sought public playgrounds so that children could have space to play. She attributed some of the lack of discipline teachers would complain about to this absence of space. "There's so little for them to do outside of school hours, except to stand around on corners and of course occasionally get into trouble just for the excitement of it. But if there were playgrounds." She was often met with resistance. Common culprits were budgets, bureaucracy and regulations. School officials also pushed back. They said they could not open the school at all hours and leave the children unsupervised.

So, she conducted an experiment. She said her staff would be glad to volunteer as inspectors to find the most effective ways of using the playground. Once they made their case for its importance to the school board, she figured they would use their own staff for the necessary supervision.

Her efforts to convince administrators at public schools to have their grounds stay open after school and during summers to serve as recreation centers was ultimately successful. Her argument that it was valuable wasted space was compelling. It took time, but by 1898, three years after the establishment of the Henry Street House, with its playground, designated New York City schools were opened as recreational centers. Public playgrounds soon followed. The Lower East Side's Seward Park was one of the first playgrounds in the United States. The *New York Times* described its setup: "There is space set aside for grass plots, stone and brick pavilion arranged for concert purposes, and finally the playground with its baths and gymnasiums. The baths are for the use of women and men as well."

Cultural Institution Accessibility

Cultural museums, like the famed Metropolitan Museum of Art, had hours and admission prices that made them inaccessible to working people. Consequently, reformers mobilized a petition campaign for the Metropolitan Museum of Art to remain open on Sundays so workers and their families could view the museum. Otherwise, the institution was in practical use only for the affluent who could afford to take off from work to visit during the week.

The petition to keep the museum open on Sundays was successful. The museum was willing to try it. It reported mixed success. On the one hand, it reported that the attendance on Sunday was "respectable, law-abiding and intelligent," with the laboring classes well represented. On the other hand, the museum was obliged to report that the Sunday opening had "offended some of the Museum's best friends and supporters leading to a loss of the bequest of $50,000."[44] The Metropolitan Opera House in the Tenderloin District became more accessible to the public as well.

Reformers sought also to improve accessibility for the working class to the outdoors and countryside. They realized that most urban children had never seen nature up close. So, they came up with a novel idea. They would have wealthy supporters open their country homes to neighborhood children.

Children who had never been outside a dense urban environment would get to spend at least a little time in nature. No longer would they be cut off from seeing plants, flowers and knowing where the food they ate came from.

Cigarette card featuring color lithograph of the Manhattan Opera House (1906), 311 West Thirty-Fourth Street, New York, between Eighth and Ninth Avenues. Cigarette cards were popular displays of cultural activities and people, such as the first baseball cards. *Wikimedia.*

Urban children needed to see "real things." One child believed that the buffalo he saw on his first visit to the zoo was the butterfly in his storybook. Another mistook a crocodile for a field mouse. So, Reverend Willard Parsons started the Fresh Air Fund by asking his congregants to open up their homes in the countryside for the summer to New York City's low-income children.

Reformers also spearheaded creating inside and outside spaces for the city's lower-class families. Jacob Riis served as the secretary of the mayor's Advisory Committee on Small Parks. Along with Lillian Wald, he promoted parks and playgrounds and helped form the Outdoor Recreation League. Funded from private donations, the league bought abandoned urban spaces and turned them into desirable locations for leisure activities like playgrounds, picnic tables and more. Their efforts also extended to indoor spaces. Skeptical of heavy alcoholic drinking and venues they felt encouraged it, the two sought to develop spaces as alternatives to saloons for social occasions. For instance, they helped raise $100,000, a large sum for 1904, to construct Clinton Hall, which offered "meeting rooms, a dance hall, restaurants, bowling alleys, and billiard rooms."[45]

ART MUSEUMS AND LIBRARIES

During the Progressive Era, a great number of cultural institutions sprang to life in New York City. Reflecting the trends of the time, most of these were funded mostly with private money. The Museum of Natural History opened around the same time with the help of Theodore Roosevelt and J.P. Morgan. This fit well into another part of the Progressive Era—passing legislation and promoting awareness on the environment. Under Teddy Roosevelt, the nascent conservationism movement was born. The aim was to preserve and open for public enjoyment forests and national parks.

The first private library in the United States opened in 1754 on Nassau Street as the New York Society Library. (George Washington was an early borrower and never returned two books. Late fees in present dollars approximate $300,000, which the library is willing to forgo.)[46] A private library, it required patrons to pay a subscription. The library relocated several times, and in 1937, it was finally moved into a mansion built twenty years before. As of this writing, it is still at that location at 53 East Seventy-Ninth Street. The New York Public Library was created as a system in 1895. The

The site of the New York Public Library at Fifth Avenue and Forty-Second Street in New York City. *Library of Congress, Prints and Photographs Division.*

New York Free Circulating Library funded no-cost reading rooms. The fact that they were free allowed theoretically anyone local to join and use them. Libraries eventually became community-centered in offering educational and literary programming besides circulating books. On a practical level, libraries offered a quiet refuge in a bustling metropolis. Branches of the library opened throughout the city, and the main building opened its doors in 1911 in a Beaux-Arts construction.

Then, there was the so-called "low brow" entertainment. Many residents had little interest in museums or libraries and preferred the wonders of Barnum's American Museum. Visitors could see live animal exhibits, wax museums, "freak shows," a zoo and natural oddities. P.T. Barnum, one of the pioneers of early circuses, ran it.

At its peak, Barnum's American Museum was open fifteen hours per day, welcoming about fifteen thousand visitors daily. It was the most popular entertainment of its day. It burned down in 1868, but it spawned a new industry of museums and exhibits of natural oddities, curiosities and wonders as mass entertainment during the Progressive Era.

Audiences also loved fantastical and nostalgic shows. A favorite in New York in the late nineteenth century was Buffalo Bill's Wild West. Buffalo Bill and Annie Oakley wowed audiences with their shooting abilities. The show promoted a mythologized or idealized view of the western frontier that was foreign and exciting to many New Yorkers. Decades later, Irving Berlin based his show *Annie Get Your Gun* on Buffalo Bill and Annie Oakley.

CENTRAL PARK

Hard-fought changes to labor laws gave workers more free time to enjoy amenities like Central Park. Others enjoyed picnics along the East River or in parks in Brooklyn. Reformers saw parks as providing not only a physical respite but also moral and cultural benefits.

The *New York Herald* printed, "When one is inclined to despair of the country, let them go to Central Park on a Saturday and spend a few hours there and look at the people. Not those who come in gorgeous carriages but those who arrive on foot or on those democratic conveyances, streetcars."

Frederick Law Olmstead and Calvin Vaux built this magnificent park in 1857, partly to provide a refuge from the bustling city. When they first envisioned Central Park, city planners could not have foreseen how dramatically the city would grow in just decades.

Central Park in 1900, as featured in the article "Central Park in Winter," by Raymond Speers, in *Munsey's Magazine* with the caption "The chinking music of the skates sings an unforgettable chant."

By the Progressive Era, Central Park had become the center of leisure for middle-class New Yorkers. The park became known as the "lungs of the city," and it became accessible to a wider range of New Yorkers. Ice skating and sleigh riding were popular winter activities, with a small amusement park and a band playing during the summer. Al Smith, a future governor of New York State, grew up in a poor tenement in the Lower East Side. He described how his friends would reach Central Park: "Our favorite way of reaching Central Park was on the open cars of the second avenue horsecar line in the summertime. They started from Fulton Ferry and gathered in all the downtown children lucky enough to get a trip to Central Park." It was said that "inscribed in Central Park was an extraordinary vision of what a great democratic city could be. But, outside its borders, tremendous tensions and conflicts remained."[47]

Pianos in Middle-Class Homes

Until the advent of the phonograph and radio, the only way the public could hear music was either by attending a live concert or by purchasing sheet music and playing the music at home or at a friend's parlor. By the late nineteenth century, the piano became a hallmark of the middle-class home. It was often one of the more expensive pieces, but householders saw it as a worthy investment. Steinway Pianos, located in Astoria, Queens, was a dominant manufacturer. Piano production nearly doubled from 1899 to 1909.[48] Phonographs rose in popularity as well. Shipments of new ones doubled during this period. Recorded music took away some of the sales from sheet music but not nearly as much as the advent of the radio a decade or so later.

This interest in music spawned an industry. There were piano teachers and, of course, writers and producers of the music itself. Tin Pan Alley,

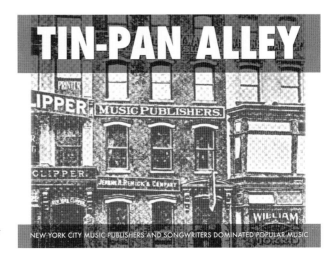

Tin Pan Alley was the center of songwriting during the Progressive Era. Located on New York's West Twenty-Eighth Street, it was said to resemble the banging of tin pans from piano players trying out new tunes. *Library of Congress, Prints and Photographs Division.*

located in Manhattan on Twenty-Eighth Street between Fifth and Sixth Avenues, was at the center of it all. It was likely named for its sounds of clanking pianos mimicking the banging of tin pans, and songwriters could be found on any day pitching their latest songs to producers, hoping they would publish their tunes on their sheet music. Five-and-dime stores commonly carried sheet music, which were known for their artful covers with beautifully drawn sketches.

Though the music sheets were cheap, pianos were not. Having a piano in a home also required space, a rare commodity in an expensive urban area. Noticing that music and other arts were increasingly common in middle-class homes but largely absent in working-class ones, reformers saw the need to include arts education for lower-income households. In Manhattan, the opening of the Educational Alliance in 1889 and the Grand Street Playhouse in 1915 created centers of arts learning for many immigrants and poor households.

INCREASED ACCESS TO LEISURE

By the second decade of the twentieth century, work hours were shorter from union demands, allowing more time for leisure pursuits. "The mean number of working hours in the unionized building trades, for instance, decreased from 48.3 per week to 44.8 in 1915."[49] Hours in manufacturing shortened from 59 to 55 during this period. Disposable income also rose. The middle class's Victorian ideals, which had always prized long work hours, now saw the value of free time. It sought, as one magazine wrote, "a middle ground between the idler and the man who works himself to death."

New technologies enabled a wider group to enjoy music, dancing and films. Most notably, Thomas Edison's kinetoscope in the 1890s brought short silent films to the public. In 1894, kinetoscope parlors opened nationally. Edison declared, "I am experimenting upon an instrument which does for the eye what the phonograph does for the ear." The kinetoscope was able to process pictures at a quick speed, creating the illusion of movement.

Later, the kinetoscopes parlors were called nickelodeons. For five cents, an audience member could view a twenty- to thirty-second silent film. In New York, the first kinetoscope parlor opened on April 14, 1894, at 1155 Broadway, near Twenty-Eighth Street. This location happened to be right by Tin Pan Alley.

Some opposed this technological development. The Victorian-esque middle class shunned the nickelodeons, as well as the first movie theaters that followed them. They saw them as places of vice. In the early days, it was largely the working class who frequented them. Eventually, movie palaces replaced nickelodeons and appealed more to middle-class sensibilities.

The first full-length feature film was the highly controversial film from D.W. Griffith, *The Birth of a Nation*, based on the book *The Clansman*. It was considered, even at that time, highly racist and was credited for awakening the dormant Ku Klux Klan. Progressive reformers fought its release. In New York, many protested the nascent movie theaters for showing it.

Despite this controversy, the movie was a financial hit. Moreover, many who had previously thumbed their noses at movie theaters started to embrace the pastime. "People who had never before dreamed of entering the portals of a motion picture theater are gazing with surprise upon the miracles unfolding before them and going away astonished at their own narrow-mindedness in the past."

Griffith felt unfairly attacked by the media for his film. As far as he was concerned, many of the so-called reformers were intolerant. As such, his subsequent film *Intolerance* showed the overreach of reformers. In one of the film's four storylines, health care advocates take away a hardworking woman's baby for no good reason. The film was a flop at the box office and drained much of Griffith's assets.

As nickelodeons and early films captured the public's attention, so did another activity—dancing. New Yorkers loved to dance the night away at dance halls. The cakewalk, turkey trot and bunny hug dominated dance music. Rag music, or ragtime, once known only in the Black community and founded by Scott Joplin, became a huge hit with mainstream audiences, ushered in by Irving Berlin's "Alexander's Ragtime Band." Journalists decried in 1909 that New York was "dance mad." Ragtime was named for its syncopated, two-beat rhythm. It was like a jagged edge. Rag music had a beat to it, and it invited dancing. In some ways, it was a forerunner of rock and roll, which was to come a half-century later.

As rag music soared in popularity, so did blues music emanating from Memphis and jazz from New Orleans. Both genres were created largely in the Black community, as was ragtime music. The largely improvisational jazz burst on the New York City scene by shaking up Harlem. It was an exciting form of "musical liberation that featured improved and blues-inflected passages played over a hot, swinging four-beat rhythm." Audiences flocked to New York dives and dance halls. Soon, the upper classes took an interest. Black entertainers were playing jazz at elite parties at homes like the Vanderbilts'.

Social class stratification existed in how New Yorkers consumed their music and dance. The wealthy frequented exclusive cabarets, while the working class filled dance halls. Of course, people had to learn to dance. So the industry of dancing schools was born. Historians estimate that in the 1910s, New York "had more than a hundred dancing schools and five hundred dance halls."[50]

People started spending more time at amusement parks like Coney Island, vaudeville, circuses, dance halls and mineral baths. Vaudeville shows provided a variety of entertainment—comics, acrobats, music players, family acts and much more. Promoters emphasized that they were family-friendly versus the rougher burlesque theaters, which had acts with more sexually provocative themes.

Coney Island was a place of leisure, escape and respite for the middle and working classes. It was a break from conventional social and romantic norms. Young men and women socialized and flirted. Performers danced provocatively. Amusement parks offered rides, minstrel shows, merry-go-rounds and wonders like big snakes and circus-like curiosities. Its popularity pointed to two trends of the late nineteenth century—first, a loosening of Victorian morals and second, more leisure outlets proliferating for the middle-class and working-class families and young singles.

Many of these societal changes were reflected in new forms of art and literature. During the mid-nineteenth century of the Gilded Age, still-lifes, portraits and impressionist art were popular. But in subsequent decades, realism emerged. It conveyed the grittiness of everyday life. Subjects included

Original Madison Square Garden in New York provided a suite of middle-class leisure activities. *New York Tribune Library of Congress, Division of Prints and Photographs.*

In 1892, Coney Island became a popular leisure destination for New York City residents. *Library of Congress, Division of Prints and Photographs.*

tenement dwellers and bar patrons, subjects who were rare in the generation before. Literature was changing, as well. Mark Twain was the catalyst. His break with tradition was the use of everyday colloquial language.

INCREASED FITNESS ACTIVITIES AND SPORTS

By the 1890s, the middle class in New York included fitness in their leisure activities. Educators also emphasized the importance of strong physical bodies. Men lifted weights. Women rode cycles. Colleges included more athletics in their curricula.

With this emphasis on physicality, the idealized forms of masculine and feminine changed too. The "Gibson Girl" became the personification of the feminine ideal of physical attractiveness. Charles Gibson created the image through a series of pen-and-ink illustrations. He viewed this image as "representing the composite of thousands of American girls."

The Gibson Girl was a composite of former American images of female beauty, such as the "fragile lady" and the "voluptuous woman." In a way, this combination personified the new middle class. The slender lines of the "fragile lady" offered respectability. The "voluptuous woman" in this version had a sexual expression but was not vulgar or lewd, as was previously depicted.

Mirroring the new middle-class values, the Gibson Girl was fashionably dressed. She was athletic. She was educated and attractive but not politically provocative. "In spirit, she was calm, independent, confident, and sought personal fulfillment. She could be depicted attending college and vying for a good mate, but she would never have participated in the suffrage movement."[51] Participating in the suffrage movement would have been associated with the new woman, a competing cultural image.

Martha Patterson's *Beyond the Gibson Girl: Reimagining the American New Woman 1895–1915* explains that the Gibson Girl undermined while simultaneously sanctioning women's desires for progressive sociopolitical change:

> *The New Woman was the more disconcerting of the two images at the time as she was seen as an example of change and disruption within the old patterns of social order, asking for the right to equal educational and work opportunities as well as progressive reform, sexual freedom, and suffrage. Whilst the Gibson Girl took on many characteristics of the New Woman, she did so without involving herself in politics and thus did not appear to be usurping traditional roles as the New Woman was deemed to. She, therefore, managed to stay within boundaries of roles without too much transgression.[52]*

A variety of women posed for Gibson illustrations. The most famous might have been Evelyn Nesbit. She was the wife of Harry Thaw, who killed the architectural genius Stanford White of the famed McKim, Mead, & White architectural firm. This iconic American image of a Gibson Girl was likely most influenced by the actress Camille Clifford, "whose high coiffure and long, elegant gowns that wrapped around her hourglass figure and tightly corseted wasp waist defined the style."[53] One illustrator went on to make *Wonder Woman* comics. Reflecting the change in taste, the Gibson Girl was featured in many places, including saucers, tablecloths, souvenir spoons and even umbrella stands.

While the Gibson Girl encapsulated the idealized woman, the strong man captured the venerated male figure. Many admired the circus performer Eugene Sandow, who immigrated to the United States in 1893 from Prussia. He was seen as the "perfect man" and the "perfect

Eugene Sandow was born to a Jewish family, though he was raised Lutheran. He left Prussia to avoid military service and became a circus strongman. He adopted his technique for popular entertainment by posing and feats of strength. Florenz Ziegfeld, one of the pioneers of the contemporary musical, realized the potential in Sandow. He noticed that audiences were more interested in Sandow's physique than the amount of weight he was lifting.

So, Ziegfeld had "Sandow move in poses which he dubbed 'muscle display performances'…and the legendary strongman added these displays in addition to performing his feats of strength with barbells. He added chain-around-the-chest breaking and other colorful displays to Sandow's routine, and Sandow quickly became Ziegfeld's first star."

The nascent film industry also gave Sandow a boost by promoting him to a wide audience. In 1894, Sandow starred in a short film series put on by the emerging Edison Studios. It was one of the first film shorts ever made. The iconic film featured Sandow flexing his muscles rather than performing any feats of physical strength. He also appeared in a brief kinetoscope film that gave rise to the first commercial motion picture exhibition in history.

He instructed on exercise, dietary habits and weight training. His advice had not been heard before and greatly impacted the physical culture. Even Buckingham Palace took notice. King George V, who had followed Sandow's teachings, appointed him as special instructor in physical culture.

gentleman." He is considered the "father of modern bodybuilding," as he transformed the way middle-class men viewed their bodies and helped spawn the fitness craze.

This change in the ideal of the body personified a greater change for the middle class. Indeed, the middle class was largely rethinking domesticity, rejecting individualism and reconsidering work and pleasure. They were molding into a new identity.[54] What that identity would become was unclear.

SPORTS

Reformers encouraged sports that promoted team building and healthy competition. As dance and jazz took off, so did baseball. It became a national pastime. In 1901, the American League was formed. Club owners built impressive stadiums. In Brooklyn, for example, Ebbets Field was built in 1913 and hosted its first game against the New York Yankees on April 5, 1913. It would be home for the Brooklyn Dodgers until the 1950s. Attendance at baseball games skyrocketed from about 800,000 in 1890 to 1.8 million in 1900. Big league game attendance spiked at 7.2 million by 1909. The baseball games started to attract female attendees, as well.

Mirroring national trends, baseball was also one of the most popular sports at the end of the nineteenth century in New York. According to several accounts, the first umpired game was played by the New York Knickerbockers versus the New York Nine in Hoboken, New Jersey, in 1846. Decades later, the New York Knickerbockers rose in popularity. Clubs formed all over Manhattan and Brooklyn. By the 1890s, the New York Giants were packing crowds at their new stadium on 155th Street and 8th Avenue. Not far away was the New York Highlanders, who were gaining ardent fans. In 1913, they were renamed the Yankees. In Brooklyn, the Bridegrooms (also nicknamed "Grays" for their uniform) in 1895 took on the nickname the Trolley Dodgers, a term used for Brooklynites.

For reformers, baseball provided a calmer and affordable leisure option. Typically, spectators cut across social classes. The *Brooklyn Daily Eagle* extolled its virtues: "Baseball is a clean and wholesome amusement, and the fact that it is not an expensive one makes its claim more deserving." In the late nineteenth century, tobacco companies packaged cigarette boxes with baseball cards. Customers sought to collect the cards for all their favorite players.

Social reformers did not see the same virtues in boxing, which was popular among the city's lower classes and not legal until 1896. Racetracks

The original Yankee Stadium in the Bronx, New York, was opened in 1923. It would be one of the most iconic structures in the game of baseball, one of the more popular leisure pursuits during the Progressive Era. The house that Babe Ruth built would last until 2009. *Wikimedia Commons.*

Jeff Tesreau, a baseball player for the New York Giants from 1912 to 1918. *Source unknown.*

were exceedingly popular among very wealthy spectators. It was a sport of contrasts. Beside the spectators and horse owners were the gamblers, who tended to be more down-and-out men. The *Cosmopolitan* described this dichotomy in 1905: "There is in the crowd a sprinkling of respectable people, lovers of outdoor sport; there is a sprinkling of more or less reputable people directly and indirectly connected with racing. And then, there are the crowds, thousands of young men neglecting their work, wasting their small earnings, preparing themselves for that desperate state of mind in which accounts are falsified, tills tapped, pockets picked and the black-jack of the highway man wielded."

It was a stratification of social classes. By the 1910s, automobile racing was also growing in popularity. In 1911, the Indy 500 was born in Indianapolis.

NEW FREEDOMS

Society's leisure offerings were changing drastically by the 1910s, thanks to the advent of motion pictures, baseball, vaudeville and music like jazz, blues and ragtime. These changes both advanced and countered reforms of the Progressive Era. This entertainment offered new freedoms for many ethnic, gender and racial groups who were largely restricted. The entertainment led to a freer identity for women and promoted individualism for many.

Many of the first baseball team owners, for example, came from the merchant or middle class. For example, the owner of the Dodgers was based in Brooklyn and originally worked as a printer. He was not from an affluent family. Many movie moguls emanated from working-class or lower-middle-class Jewish families. Sam Goldwyn, of the famed MGM, emerged from the garment business.

Black performers crossed racial boundaries by performing for White audiences in music, theater and sports. Jack Johnson, for example, a heavyweight boxing champion in 1908, was largely watched by White audiences. The same was true for many Black performers in jazz, like Jelly Roll Morton. However, racial boundaries were still clear. In many cases, venue owners denied Black performers accommodations in White hotels and restaurants.

Some of these new music venues and sporting games allowed more social and racial integration. Jazz served as a vehicle for Black and White artists to play together. But this tolerance had its limits. Vaudeville theaters banned Black attendees or required them to sit in the balcony. Major league baseball teams would not recruit Black players. Moreover, Black people were often denied entrance in amusement parks and were kept out of many dance halls.

With much of this new entertainment at a low cost, it became in reach for working-class families. Vaudeville tickets, nickelodeons and circus performances were more affordable than theater or opera tickets. Suddenly, paid performances became something individuals from lower-income families attended.

These new forms of entertainment encouraged more inter-class mingling and access, which was a goal of Progressives. Yet many of these venues promoted freer attitudes about sexuality, which flew in the face of some Victorian-ideal reformers. "At a time when reformers tried to restrain sexual behavior in general, and prostitution in particular, vaudeville, amusement parks, dances, songs, and movies offered a more relaxed and open approach to sex. For instance, Vaudeville theaters featured well-known women swimmers posing in their bathing suits."[55] The music industry pumped out songs with sexual themes, like "In My Merry Oldsmobile."

Americans were coy about discussing sexual issues in public, and reformers worked to decrease unplanned pregnancy. In New York, a few reformers like Margaret Sanger, a former nurse, published controversial articles in New York newspapers. Hers was called "What Every Girl Should Know." She emphasized the need for birth control and argued the merits of contraception not only for family planning but also for couples to enjoy sex without having to worry about unplanned pregnancies. It was a revolutionary and hotly contested position. Sanger went against the moral code espoused by many Progressives.

While not embraced by many reformers, Sanger's articles brought forth new notions of sexual freedom in urban centers like New York City. In many communities, there was also limited toleration of homosexuality. The gay community in New York expanded from the Bowery to Greenwich Village in the 1910s. The Village began gaining a reputation as a home for those who rejected conventionality, such as marriage and materialism, and who tended to perform jobs that were more creative than remunerative. Later, during Prohibition, the Village was also home to many speakeasies. This flouting of laws, along with a bohemian attitude, increased the presence for those outside the mainstream, including gay and lesbian people. In a de facto segregated city, Harlem was the only place where Black gay men could congregate at various venues. In subsequent decades, many were key in the Harlem Renaissance, with participation in literary circles, blues clubs and basement speakeasies.

PUSHBACK ON MORALS OF LEISURE

With this new leisure and sexual freedom came a pushback. Clergy, club women, politicians and reformers questioned the morals of sports, amusement parks, birth control, dance halls and, most of all, movies. Some decried the "pernicious moving picture abomination" that was "recruiting stations of vice." Detractors cautioned that movie theaters would encourage poor people to waste their pennies and would encourage inappropriate relations between boys and girls and the stirring up of "primitive passion."

Therefore, some reformers in New York were interested not only in changing society with advances in worker rights and women's suffrage, among others, but also in interfering with people's personal lives. For these reformers, modifications to the external world were insufficient. To enact long-lasting

"Woman, keep away from that big city chap." "Miss Democracy," an elderly lady with corkscrew curls and glasses, clad in an old-fashioned full-length bathing suit, standing on the beach admiring Governor Al Smith of New York, who strikes a heroic pose in a bathing suit. William Jennings Bryan admonishes her to "keep away from that big city chap." Smith was one of the two prime candidates for the Democratic presidential nomination in 1924. Some saw Smith as the exemplar of all they distrusted—cities, anti-Prohibition and business and financial interests. *Courtesy Library of Congress, Division of Prints and Photographs.*

One example of a reformer pushing puritanical ideals was Belle Moskowitz. A social worker at the Educational Alliance, a Jewish Settlement on the Lower East Side of Manhattan, Moskowitz would become one of the most politically influential women in the United States, according to her *New York Times* obituary. She and her second husband, Harry Moskowitz, advocated strongly for commercial dance hall regulation. She was one of New York governor Al Smith's key advisors. Both she and Governor Smith were strong social reformers. She was responsible for helping contain tuberculosis, protecting children from labor exploitation and funding public parks and playgrounds. She enacted many of the reforms for textile workers after the Triangle Shirtwaist fire.

She sounded the alarm on unchaperoned girls being led astray. She was particularly wary of dance halls and was concerned about their serving of liquor and the young women being exploited for sex. She discovered that Tammany Hall officials were behind much of this corruption. She strong-armed many to pass laws outlawing drinking and sex in dance halls. The *New York Times* noted, "These laws did more to improve the moral surroundings of young girls than any other single social reform of the period."

transformations, they felt people must avoid drinking, divorce, prostitution and leisure activities, which might stir the wrong passions.

Lawmakers in New York State and New York City bowed to reforms demanded by church leaders. They applied Sunday closing laws to movie theaters. They also banned children not present with adults. Some movie theaters tried compromising. For example, some New York–based movie theaters agreed to submit new films to a National Board of Censorship of Programs of Motion Picture shows. The board allowed characters to struggle with various conflicts so long as the film's end was "appropriate." This decision meant wrongdoing was not rewarded. Al Smith would play an important role in these legislative decisions. In some ways, there was a marked contrast between values of urban versus rural New York voters.

In the end, many of these efforts backfired. Some Progressives disagreed with interfering in people's personal affairs and ways they spent their leisure time. Others saw great promise in new forms of entertainment. The middle class, which emanated largely from the Progressive Era, started to question these motives as well. Transitioning from Victorian ideals, some of the new middle class started to be more open to new leisure pursuits and less strict about social and sexual norms. This new morality seemed out of step. Many middle-class reformers turned their attention to gaining more rights for women.

Part IV

Rights for Women and Black People

WOMEN'S SUFFRAGE

WORKING WOMEN

The *New York Herald* in 1869 observed that one-fourth of all women in New York performed paid work. Many of these were young, unmarried and working-class women. For most of them, their labor participation was not a political statement but an economic reality. They needed the income.

Working women changed the look of New York City. According to New York history writer Esther Crain, "They crowded into streetcars and elevated railroads during rush hour, clad in flimsy dresses or shirtwaists, clutching an overhead strap in one hand and a dime novel in the other. They stopped for a sandwich at the new quick-lunch counters popping up in the city. If they didn't live in a tenement, they rented a room in a women's boardinghouse or working women's residences."[56]

In the early twentieth century, the "new woman" emerged. She held different values and even looked different from her Victorian-era mother. Even habits like smoking were changing. Formerly, it was exclusively men who smoked. Alarmed at this trend, in 1908, New York City officials considered an ordinance to ban smoking for women. The Board of Aldermen did pass a municipal law in New York City on January 21, 1908, which "barred the management of a public place from allowing women to smoke within their venue." Confusingly, this allowed women to smoke, both in private and in public.

National Women's Trade Union League in 1903 was fighting for an eight-hour workday, framed as important so that the women laborers could "guard their home." *Wikimedia,* Life and Labor *magazine.*

As women played a larger role in the workplace, many experienced discrimination, low and unequal pay, dangerous conditions and poor treatment. Therefore, some women laborers fought for better working conditions. The formation of the International Ladies' Garment Workers Union in 1900 was a turning point for women's labor movements. Before, many unions had shut out or had not taken as equals women and unskilled laborers.

One influential figure, Clara Lemlich, a Ukrainian worker, gave a rousing speech at Cooper Union in November 1909, calling on the audience to take action with strikes. Ironically, the group called for a general strike against the Triangle Waist Company. Over twenty thousand fellow garment industry workers walked off the job. It was known as the New York Shirtwaist Strike. The company offered few concessions. It did agree to not charge workers for the supplies and to create a fifty-two-hour workweek. However, on March 25, 1911, the site would become the worst disaster in New York City industrial history. The fire caused the deaths of 146 garment workers, mostly young immigrant women, from inhaling smoke or falling or jumping to their deaths. The owners locked the floors, so many workers could not escape in time.

WOMEN'S SUFFRAGE IN NEW YORK STATE

New York State was central in the fight for women's suffrage. During the 1830s and 1840s, women and some men had been discussing laws about property and inheritance rights based on gender. These and many other grievances had a formal structure at the Seneca Falls Convention of 1848. Held on July 19–20, 1848, in Seneca Falls, New York, located near Rochester, the convention was the first women's rights assembly in the United States and launched a movement. Elizabeth Cady Stanton, one of the organizers, declared the meeting's purpose on the first day: "We are assembled to protest against a form of government, existing without the consent of the governed—to declare our right to be free as man is free, to be represented in the government which we are taxed to support, to have such disgraceful laws as give man the power to chastise and imprison his wife, to take the wages which she earns, the property which she inherits, and, in case of separation, the children of her love."

The convention stated its Declaration of Sentiments to call on women to fight for their constitutionally guaranteed right to equality as U.S. citizens.

The New York Capitol in Albany, New York, was completed in 1899 in the Romanesque Revival and Neo-Renaissance styles. It was one of the most expensive government buildings of its time. *Wikimedia Commons, by Beyond My Ken.*

The declaration delineated nineteen "abuses and usurpations" of women's exclusion in voting, education and the church. The eleven resolutions demanded equal rights in a variety of fields, including the most controversial: the ability to vote. That declaration led many women's right proponents to withdraw their support.

Many of the initial organizers were also abolitionists, a movement that took great courage and often put oneself or one's family in danger. These women included Lucretia Mott, Mary McClintock, Martha Wright and Jane Hunt.

In subsequent years, supporters campaigned for women's rights at statewide and federal events. Speakers sometimes referenced that Declaration of Sentiments.

Changes came slowly over the next sixty-five years. But by 1915, the movement had accelerated. New York rose "to a height never attained elsewhere and culminated in two campaigns that in number of adherents and comprehensive work were never equaled."[57]

In January 1915 in Albany, both houses of the legislature in New York State voted to submit the issue of women's right to vote to the public on a referendum for the general election that fall. The Women's Political Union in New York City knew it had a short time to influence the voters. Leaders gave matinee talks every day. Both pro- and anti-suffrage movements saw this time as critical.

Not all publications supported the women's suffrage movement. The *New York Times* and *Ladies' Home Journal*, for example, did not. The latter commissioned major anti-suffrage investigations by journalist Richard Barry. The *New York Times* ran an editorial on February 6, 1915, titled, "It Must Be Defeated."

THE SUFFRAGENTS

Lesser known were the male suffragists who ardently supported women's right to vote. New York City was a center for that movement. On May 6, 1911, the second annual New York Suffrage parade marched down Fifth Avenue. Among the participants were eighty-nine men who were part of the Men's League for Woman Suffrage. These men included titans of publishing, industry, science, academia and the clergy. Since the end of 1909, they had been "speaking, writing, editing, or publishing, planning, and lobbying New York's governor and legislators on behalf of the suffrage cause. They did so

President Woodrow Wilson as a prospector with a pickaxe labeled "Statesmanship," leading the Democratic donkey loaded with a "Social Justice Program" up a hill labeled "The New Order." Probably refers to the liberal social program adopted by Wilson and the Democrats in 1916. *Lute Pease, Library of Congress, Prints and Photographs Division.*

until the vote was won."[58] W.E.B. Du Bois and Stephen Wise were among them. Many would also later fight for the advancement of Black Americans and against entry into the Great War.

As the men paraded by, onlookers sneered at them, saying, "Hold up your skirts, girls!" and "You won't get any dinner unless you march all the way!"

President Woodrow Wilson declined to support the suffrage movement. He commented to his friend Nancy Saunders Toy, "Suffrage for women will make absolutely no change in politics—it is the home that will be disastrously affected. Somebody has to make the home and who is going to do it if the women don't?"

Path to Victory

After a year of campaigning by both sides, in November, voters defeated the measure. In fact, only five New York counties passed it. But the suffragents and suffragettes fought on.

They pressured Woodrow Wilson and local congress members into supporting a constitutional amendment for women's right to vote. On the state level, New York State passed the measure by the needed two-thirds majority for two consecutive years. This measure allowed for a new voter referendum in November 1917.

Harriot Blatch, daughter of famed original suffragette Elizabeth Cady Stanton, joined a delegation to meet Wilson on July 24. She told him:

> *What an uphill, fruitless battle so far the New York State amendment fight had been. I am sixty years old. I have worked all my life for suffrage, and I am determined that I will never again stand up on the street corners of a great city appealing to every Tom, Dick, and Harry for the right of self-government. When we work for a Federal Amendment, we are dealing at last with men who understand what we are talking about and can speak to us in our own tongue. We are asking for a dignified way, and we ought to be able to rely on the chivalry of our representatives…to accord to women a self-respecting method of working out their enfranchisement.*[59]

But Woodrow Wilson was not deterred from his stance. He worried about upsetting his party, particularly in the South. He noted that the "Negro question," that is the White fear of a Black voting majority in the South, was the primary impediment. Blatch countered that his lack of

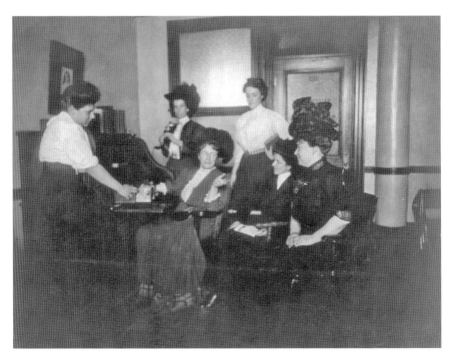

Harriot Blatch meets with suffragettes to strategize on gaining more support. *Library of Congress, Division of Prints and Photographs.*

support would mean losing women's vote in western states, where women did have the right to vote.

As the Great War wore on, Wilson changed his stance. After his narrow reelection, he addressed the Gridiron Club on why the movement for women's suffrage was becoming appealing. He emphasized the problems of "how to work out common rights." He stated, "Women feel further than we do and feeling, if it be comprehending, feeling goes further in the solution of problems than cold thinking does. The day of cold thinking, of fine-spun constitutional argument, is gone, thank God. We do not now discuss so much what the Constitution of the United States is as what the constitution of human society is. And we know in our hearts that, if we ever find a place or a time where the Constitution of the United States is contrary to the constitution of human nature and human society, we have got to change [it]."[60]

This attitude was a shift in thinking. Wilson was advocating for taking into account human feelings and needs—not just rational facts and data. By January 1917, he told reporters he supported suffrage and wanted it enacted imminently. For a while, Wilson was essentially playing both sides of the debate. But Wilson admired many suffragettes, and they ultimately influenced his thinking on the hot-button issue. Moreover, he had promised that the Great War would restore democracy globally. To deny women the vote seemed counter to that objective. Wilson relented.

As the vote for suffrage in New York State neared, periodicals like the *New York Tribune* endorsed it, partly on the grounds of the service suffragettes had been offering during the war. The newspaper noted, "Women were not seeking the ballot as a reward for the patriotic service they had provided but as a further means of rendering service." The New York State Woman Suffrage Committee cleverly placed a two-column ad in many newspapers the day before the election, highlighting the support for suffrage from key male political and economic figures.

On Election Day, the fate was sealed. Voters passed the New York State amendment in a "sweeping victory," which gave the right to vote to every eligible female citizen in New York over the age of twenty-one as of January 1, 1918. It was the fourteenth state to endorse women's suffrage but one of the only ones in the East.

A day after this stunning victory, suffragettes celebrated at the historic Cooper Union. Nearly six decades before, it had been the site of presidential candidate Abraham Lincoln's Cooper Union Speech. That speech would propel him to the Republican nomination. The day after women's suffrage passed in New York State, Cooper Union saw one of its largest—and loudest—gatherings. Amid this festivity, participants sifted through returns and came up with plans for the "next step in the battle."

The unprecedented organizing efforts in New York paid off. Through picketing, advocating, partnering with men supporters and gaining key endorsements, they overcame the 1915 loss of an 82,755 vote margin against suffrage.

Former president Theodore Roosevelt was very pleased with the election results as well. He said, "The women deserved it, they were entitled to it, and I am glad the voters saw it as they should. The vote for suffrage has grown wonderfully, and the vote of yesterday is an honor to every man who marked his ballot for women." In addition to his other contributions to the campaign, he must have done some local lobbying, because the measure passed 272 to 70 at his polling place in Oyster Bay.[61]

Carrie Chapman Catt, president of the National American Woman Suffrage Association and founder of the League of Women Voters and the International Alliance of Women, shortly after victory, reflected on this win for future generations: "Mayors come, and mayors may go. A hundred years from now, the deeds of the present-day mayors will have been forgotten. But the children of the centuries to come will learn that on November 6, 1917, a great step for human freedom was accomplished in the State of New York. I want to give our heartfelt thanks to the men who voted for suffrage; and to those who voted 'No' I want to say that we won fairly and squarely. Be good sports now and accept us into the fraternity of democracy."[62]

The rally opened with the "Star-Spangled Banner" and closed with the "Battle Hymn of the Republic." But, somehow, the lyrics seemed different now.

Now the question was how to pass a constitutional amendment. Leaders would need to get Congress to pass with thirty-six of the then forty-eight states to ratify outlawing gender discrimination at voting sites across the United States. The group vowed that they "shall never rest till every woman in the whole U.S. in enfranchised."

At another celebration at the Ritz Carlton hotel, Dudley Malone addressed the five hundred participants. His father was a Tammany Hall official, and Malone was born into Democratic politics. He was perhaps most famous at the time as a campaign manager for Woodrow Wilson's presidential run. However, in his political career—and as a New York State governor hopeful—he took on a less orthodox position. He broke decisively from the Wilson administration due to its opposition to suffrage, as well as other issues.

In reflecting on the victory, New York State suffrage activists noted the success of picketing: "The very substantial victory we have won in New York

Suffragette parade where women and some men known as "suffragents" demanded a constitutional amendment. *Library of Congress, Division of Prints and Photographs.*

is not due to the belated efforts of the gentlemen of the Cabinet, but to the men and women in New York who love liberty. But it cannot be denied that the women who dared by their picketing to dramatize the injustice done American women did much to aid in winning the victory."[63]

Malone reminded the crowd that they must stand in unison along with their male supporters—but "don't sweetly ask for anything. Demand it."[64]

In subsequent weeks and months, suffragettes kept the pressure on Wilson and his administration. By January 9, 1918, reeling from the Great War, Wilson met with the Democratic members of the House suffrage committee. The *New York Times* reported, "Wilson backs amendment for woman suffrage." The Democrats crafted a carefully worded statement. It read, "The committee found that the President had not felt at liberty to volunteer his advice to members of Congress in this important matter, but when we sought his advice he very frankly and earnestly advised us to vote for the amendment as an act of right and justice to the women of the country and of the world."[65]

As noted earlier, Wilson's advocacy for suffrage was tepid. But by December 1918, he was more direct in his support. Perhaps uncoincidentally, his full support came just three weeks after the allies signed the armistice with Germany that ended the fighting on the Western Front.

He proclaimed as part of a longer speech, "The least tribute we can pay them [women] is to make them equals of men in political rights as they have proved themselves their equals in every field of practical work they have entered, whether for themselves or for their country. These great days of completed achievement would be sadly marred were we to omit that act of justice."

On June 4, 1919, both houses of Congress passed the Susan B. Anthony Amendment. Fourteen months later, the requisite 75 percent of states ratified it. Finally, suffragettes had achieved their aim set about at a controversial meeting in Seneca Falls, New York, seventy-two years before.

How did this happen after almost three-quarters of a century? The United States entry into the Great War was a major factor. It gave moral standing to suffragettes. If women had to risk their husbands and/or sons' lives but had no say in the war policy, how was that fair? If the United States claimed it was making the world safe for democracy abroad, how could it deny half its citizens the right to vote—let alone civil rights? Suffragettes exposed the government's hypocrisy.

During the war, women played a key role in the workplace by filling in gaps left by men who went to fight overseas. Others played critical roles in nursing soldiers. In doing so, they garnered "street cred" with much of the electorate. Society began to see the role of women differently. Another factor was the strong advocacy through picketing and lobbying efforts.

On a political level, the amendment probably passed due to Wilson finally supporting it. Also, Congress members representing states and districts where women already had the vote were concerned that their lack of support for the suffrage amendment could cost them in future elections. Indeed, more than 90 percent of representatives and senators from suffrage states supported the federal amendment. This stands in contrast with the 50 percent of those from non-suffrage states.[66]

Brooke Kroeger's *The Suffragents* explains the momentum that was built starting in 1917: "In the closing months of 1917, the late-breaking addition of increasing support from the largest delegation in the House of Representatives—that of New York, with its 43 seats—provided unmistakable help in tipping the congressional balance. Oklahoma, Michigan, and South Dakota all supplied a boost as their state amendments passed in 1918.... State-by-state initiatives were needed to continue in tandem with the federal suffrage campaign. At the same time, the support for the federal amendment from legislators from non-suffrage states also increased steadily, indicating the general change in attitude towards the federal measure."[67]

The passage of the Nineteenth Amendment was surely one of the great and last accomplishments of reformers. Efforts began in the early nineteenth century, but it was during the Progressive Era that the movement picked up steam and ultimately crossed the finish line.

While some suffragettes played important roles in securing equal rights for Black people, many White reformers did little to help the cause. The longtime struggle for racial equality would fall largely on Black reformers.

9

RACIAL DIVIDE

W hite social reformers generally did not emphasize racial equality in their list of priorities during the Progressive Era. There were exceptions, like Jane Addams and Lillian Wald, both settlement house pioneers who held racially integrated classes. The seed for what would become the NAACP was planted in the dining room of Lillian Wald's Henry Street Settlement.

William Walling, another New York settlement house resident, socialist and journalist, was an ardent supporter of Black rights. He wrote, "We must come to treat the Negro on a plane of absolute political and social equality."

Sadly, many White reformers did little to advance racial equality. Many saw racial divides as a fact of life and that little could be done about it. Others, like Woodrow Wilson, carried out racist policies. Some also promoted eugenics and the genetic superiority of western Europeans versus eastern and southern Europeans, as well as Black people. Indeed, eugenics was an ugly and often overlooked part of some of the Progressive reformers' agendas. Historians estimate that in 1920 there were 376 courses devoted to eugenics. Some strongly advocated quotas on immigrants from eastern and southern Europe, branding them as genetically inferior.

Social gospel leader Josiah Strong, for instance, believed in the superiority of Anglo-Saxons. He asked, "Is there room for doubt that this race is destined to dispossess many weaker races, assimilate others, and mold the remainder until it has Anglo-Saxonized mankind?"

Teddy Roosevelt also held condescending views towards Black people. He told a friend in 1906 that "as a race and in the mass they are altogether inferior to the whites." He opted not to intervene in racial lynchings, Jim Crow laws, systematic disenfranchisement and institutionalized segregation gripping the South. Instead, he felt the South should work it out itself. He was wary of alienating voters in the South. When Roosevelt invited Booker T. Washington to the White House in 1901, he was torn to shreds by southern newspapers. His successor, William Taft, continued Roosevelt's method of letting the South deal with its racial strife itself. Taft opted to not intervene.

While Roosevelt and Taft were passive about segregation, Woodrow Wilson legislated discriminatory measures. Elected with White southern votes, he "allowed several federal departments to segregate their black employees in Washington and demote or fire black federal workers in the South."[68]

Many Progressives did not speak out about racial disharmony. They were more interested in middle-class reform. Michael McGerr's *A Fierce Discontent: The Rise and Fall of the Progressive Movement in America* reflects on this paradox:

> *The Progressive support for the different forms of Jim Crow was a critical moral blunder. Segregation certainly reflected the power of progressives and other privileged whites, but it also revealed their weakness. The rise of progressivism represented a remarkable reworking of middle-class ideology, a creative deployment of a host of devices for reform, and a bold determination to take on some of the most basic and intractable issues of human existence. Willing to believe that a kind of paradise might really be attainable someday, progressives showed little fear in dealing with problems of gender, family, class, and economy—but not of race.*[69]

Thomas Leonard, a research scholar in the Humanities Council and a lecturer in economics at Princeton University and author of *Illiberal Reformers: Race, Eugenics & American Economics in the Progressive Era*, also wrote about this "darker history of racism and xenophobia among its politicians." He wrote, "The industrial revolution and the rise of big business after 1870 dramatically increased American living standards, but the era was plagued by recurring financial crises, violent labor conflicts, and two deep economic contractions. In response, Progressive economists sought to regulate the American economy through a new administrative state based on scientific management principles. They established economics as an academic discipline while promoting and helping build regulatory and independent institutions."[70]

Leonard shows, however, that their policies were "undergirded by social Darwinism and eugenics and excluded groups deemed inferior—including women, Southern- and Eastern-European immigrants, Catholics, Jews, and blacks." He continued, "They wanted to help 'the people,' but excluded millions of Americans from that privileged category on the grounds that they were inferior." In conducting his research, Leonard noted that he was "forced to confront the fact that race and social science intersected in complicated ways. The entanglement was significant and deeply rooted in the Progressive Era."[71]

The most notable example is that southern Progressives threw up a series of obstacles for Black people to register to vote, including difficult literacy tests and unaffordable poll taxes. By excluding Black people from voting by these onerous measures, the Jim Crow laws were kept intact.

Some justified these actions with the new "science" of eugenics. The field started winning more support. For example, by 1910, Teddy Roosevelt offered his support to this pseudoscience. Eugenics advocates encouraged reproduction of people with "desirable traits" and discouraging reproduction of those with "unwanted traits." One example was the eugenics movement's strong advocacy for the sterilization of mental institution inmates, even if against the patient's will.

BLACK ACTIVISTS DURING THE PROGRESSIVE ERA

It was through the efforts of Black social reformers that progress was made. Many protested the rampant lynching that had gripped the South since the 1870s. Those responsible for lynching were often poor White people and, unfortunately, law enforcement officers. It is estimated that "between 1882 and 1910, at least 2,500 blacks were lynched. During the 1890s, lynchings soared to about 187 a year, or roughly one killing every two days."[72]

Mary Church Terrell and Ida Wells-Barnett, an outspoken journalist, brought awareness to this gruesome practice where Black people were hanged for trumped-up causes or minor offenses. Very few received fair trials. Perpetuators knew that the killings might arouse opposition. So, they disguised the reasons for the lynchings as being revenge for sexual assaults by Black men against White women. In some cases, these trumped up charges were falsified.

Wells investigated the matter and discovered that the real reason for lynching was to instill fear and submission. In most cases, no crime was committed. Risking her life, Wells published her findings in a pamphlet titled *Southern Horrors: Lynch Law in All Its Phases.* Some northerners began to recoil at the injustice. Some politicians introduced anti-lynching bills in Congress;

however, southern opposition soundly defeated them. But it helped bring about more activism for equal rights.

Black reformers differed on the speed and manner in which they believed equal rights should be sought. On the one hand, there was the famed Booker T. Washington, president of the Tuskegee Institute in Alabama. He favored a more calculated approach of educating Black people so that they would "quietly elevate themselves."

W.E.B. Du Bois and Ida Wells strongly disagreed with this approach. They believed that fervent and immediate action was needed—not accommodation. Du Bois studied at Fisk University and was the first Black student to obtain a PhD. As part of his activism, W.E.B. Du Bois organized a meeting in Niagara Falls, New York, to reject the accommodation of segregation.

Ida Wells in a photograph by Mary Garrity in 1893. Wells exposed the brutal lynchings of Black men throughout the South. *Wikimedia Commons.*

The Niagara Movement, as it came to be known, rejected accommodation of southern White people, protested disfranchisement, advocated for industrial education and economic self-help. The meeting proclaimed, "We do not hesitate to complain and to complain loudly and insistently."

The group had a good start but stalled due to monetary constraints. Race riots were brewing across the United States. Liberal White people started to notice Du Bois and Wells's cause, and an impetus was growing. From this early movement eventually sprang the founding of the NAACP. The group protested Wilson's firing of Black employees and federal government segregation rules. It also sought to weaken Jim Crow laws in the courts.

GREAT MIGRATION TO THE NORTH AND IN NEW YORK CITY

Though segregation was far more severe in the South, many northern institutions did not welcome Black people. Some communities kept Black people out of hotels, restaurants, theaters, parks and other public facilities. Some churches rejected Black worshippers.

Still, the North provided Black southerners a way to sidestep Jim Crow laws and to try to escape poverty. Therefore, the Great Migration from the rural South to the urbanized North started in the late nineteenth century, with an acceleration in the 1910s and 1920s.

A significant percentage ended up in New York City. Shut out of many neighborhoods, Black residents found it easier to rent apartments in Harlem. Mary Ovington, a cofounder of the NAACP, described the dirty tenements Black people were relegated to as "human hives, honeycombed with little rooms thick with human beings." They lived among housing stock that few others wanted, including the Tenderloin district near present-day Penn Station.

Lorraine Diehl's *Late, Great Pennsylvania Station* describes the Tenderloin neighborhood in stark terms:

> *The edifice of poverty is a death mask, neither reflecting life nor recording its disintegration, and in 1901 the West Side of Manhattan…was a Dickensian landscape of piano factories, stockyards, and slaughterhouses. Rows of tenements housed people who lived amid the stench of slaughtered pigs and cattle. Thirty-Ninth Street was nicknamed Pig Alley. Above the streets, an ever-present dense gray cloud of soot, spewed from the chimneys of freighters and ocean liners that clogged the piers, darkened the sun. It mixed with coal smoke from freight trains that ran along Eleventh Avenue and from the elevated trains that ran above Ninth.*[73]

Moreover, nearby Eleventh Avenue was known as Death Avenue for the storming of the New York Central freight line up and down Tenth and Eleventh Avenue killing and maiming bystanders, often children, in its wake. (Paradoxically, the track above this area is now the pedestrian-friendly and environmentally conscious High Line.) An 1892 *New York World* article referred to the trains as "monsters which menaced them [neighborhood residents] night and day." A *New York Times* article claimed that in the 1890s, there had been about two hundred deaths, many of whom were children.

To ameliorate this situation, the city had a novel idea. It hired cowboys to ride in front of trains to warn bystanders to stand back. The ordinance read that it "shall employ a proper person to precede the trains on horseback, to give the necessary warning in a suitable manner on their approach."[74] Thus the lore of the urban cowboy was born. Archival photos show cowboys on horses in front of trains on Eleventh Avenue. They were known as the West Side Cowboys. They waved red flags by day and lanterns by night to warn

Eleventh Avenue, with train, often called "Death Avenue" for the storming of the New York Central freight, killing and maiming bystanders, often children, in its wake. *Courtesy Library of Congress, Division of Prints and Photographs.*

street dwellers of an impending train. The results were mixed. The railroad continued to be a menace.[75]

After the opening of the subway line to 145th Street, a Black relator, Philip Payton Jr., encouraged Black people to move to Harlem. The neighborhood had become a hotbed for Jewish people fleeing the crowded Lower East Side. However, White landlords were not filling their brownstones fast enough. Financial woes followed. Therefore, the sellers and buyers were motivated. There was a strong demand for tenants in Harlem, and Black residents needed higher-quality living accommodations. Payton assisted residents in moving from Midtown to the more accommodating Harlem apartments.

Payton persuaded Black investors to purchase the property. He did so by appealing to their business sense: "Today is the time to buy if you want to be numbered among those of the race who are doing something toward trying to solve the so-called 'Race Problem.'" Payton's Afro-American Realty company brochure stated that "race prejudice is a luxury, and, like all other luxuries, can be made very expensive in New York City. The very prejudice which has heretofore worked against us can be turned and used to our profit."[76]

Payton's entrepreneurial instincts, along with racism among landlords and an oversupply of unsold and unrented buildings in Harlem, resulted in about 70 percent of New York City's Black population moving to Harlem. Soon after, in the 1920s, the Harlem Renaissance, with jazz clubs, dance halls, blues music and more would usher in the golden age of Harlem.

While activists were fighting for civil liberties for Black people and women, they turned their attention to businesses and demanded far better working conditions. They used a new tool—labor strikes—to bring about changes. Sadly, though, many unions would keep out women, Black men and unskilled laborers.

Part V

BUSINESS AND GOVERNMENT REFORMS

Unions and Strikes

New technology changed New York workers' lives. They were expected to produce more in less time. Mechanization created a need for less skilled labor, yielding lower wages and longer hours. Any worker who complained was easily replaced. In the textile and garment trades, as a result of automation, far fewer workers were needed per output piece. Many toiled for twelve hours per day for six days a week for unlivable wages. New Yorkers had to fill the gap of their low income and expenses by taking in boarders and yanking their children out of school to send them off to work, even illegally. Parents often ignored state child protection laws and gave them up to production managers who were usually interested solely in profits and production quotas.

Many workers complained about task monotony. They were demoralized by pulling levers and doing little else. It was boring work. As a result of this tediousness, workers made errors and created safety hazards. The clock dominated the day. Workers arriving late or taking unauthorized breaks could be fired. Most workers never met their company's owners. Instead, they reported to foremen, many of whom were abusive.

Reformers saw improving conditions for workers as one of their key goals. During the Progressive Era, there was an unprecedented number of strikes resulting from solidarity among workers. However, the company versus union story is more nuanced. Unions themselves were often divided by race, gender and skill. Many unions did not accept female workers for fear they would drag wages down. Many also did not accept Black or unskilled workers based on racism and a belief that unskilled work was not worthy of the same protections as work requiring technical skill.

LABOR STRIKES

During the Gilded Age, as expectations of worker output rose, wages generally did not. As a result, a rift widened between employers and employees. New York owners felt they had a right to run their businesses as they saw fit. Workers pushed back. Until the Progressive Era, many workers did not assert their rights. But in the wake of the industrial age, employees began to consider striking—so did unemployed laborers.

Hundreds of labor union activists were arrested in New York and in other cities. They were charged with conspiracy and trying to destroy private property, meaning private businesses. Judges were generally unsympathetic to workers' causes.

Parade of the Unemployed in May 1909, showing unemployed yet unified workers. *Wikimedia Commons.*

The Conference Committee of the Unemployed of New York carries a banner to air their frustrations and grievances of pervasive unemployment. *Library of Congress Division of Prints and Photographs.*

For many New York State employers, as well as those around the nation, these labor strikes were cause for concern. They believed that organized labor and collective bargaining would undermine their businesses. Some also felt union leaders were corrupt or were misleading their members. Indeed, industrial output decreased as a result of unions during this period, according to a 1907 federal report. Anarchist marches also contributed to the fearful climate.

Employers grew alarmed. Between 1880 and 1900, the United States experienced about thirty-seven thousand strikes, even if some were small and local. The volume of strikes rocked the nation's workforce. Even more dramatic was the large number of bombings that targeted businesses and anti-labor organizations. Some saw these bombings as proof that labor unions were violent, although almost all strike violence was caused by police and militia brought in to break strikes. The intention was to scare not only strikers but also onlooking frightened Americans.

While President Theodore Roosevelt was understanding of workers, he questioned the closed-shop system under which workers were forced to join unions. As a strong proponent of individual values, he opposed mandatory unions.

SCIENTIFIC MANAGEMENT

To combat decreases in output caused partly by organized unions, management experimented with various ways of incentivizing workers. Some were by the carrot and others by the stick. On the carrot side was the idea of welfare capitalism. Employers following this system were generally more benevolent toward their employees. They offered an array of benefits and sometimes even limited stock in the company.

But others were skeptical of this arrangement. They wanted to cajole workers to optimize their output. This trend was scientific management. The "pioneers of systematic management favored piece-rate schemes that would encourage workers to defy their formal and informal working rules and increase production."[77]

Frederick Taylor was one of its biggest advocates. Taylor grew up in a well-to-do family but ended up in a working-class setting. That influenced some of his outlook and later his obsessive drive for industrial productivity. Born to an affluent Quaker family in Philadelphia, Taylor suffered from several illnesses. He ended up becoming a machinist and pattern maker and saw firsthand the inner workings of the shop floor. He advanced to becoming an engineering consultant and inventor of machine tools. He wondered what factors would make manufacturing more efficient. The industrial engineer envisioned a more scientific management system and published the influential book *Shop Management*.

Taylor subscribed to the rugged individualism of the time. He praised "energy, grit, pluck, determination, ability to stick to it, and character." But he lacked empathy for workers. For him, they were essentially paid cogs in a system to maximize output and return on investment for labor and capital for the owners. Anything outside of that philosophy, he saw as superfluous. He called welfare capitalism "a joke and of secondary importance." Instead, he favored a survival-of-the-fittest model. Workers were compensated by piecemeal output. Those who could produce more would be offered additional compensation. Those who under-produced would see their pay cut. The theory held that the less productive workers would clear out over time, leaving a more efficient labor pool.

In Taylor's book *The Principles of Scientific Management*, he presented his productivity laws: "It is only through enforced standardization of methods, enforced adoption of the best implements and working conditions, and enforced cooperation that this faster work can be assured. And the duty of enforcing the adoption of standards and enforcing this cooperation rests with management alone."

Taylor was not content to verify the final output of workers, though. He wanted to investigate *how* they achieved their output. His motion study was a detailed observation of each minute aspect of a task. He broke each sub-task the worker did into pieces. He used a stopwatch to establish the optimal time for each of these sub-tasks. He and others developed mathematical formulas to find the right time workers would perform each task. The approach treated each worker as interchangeable and like a human machine. Indeed, Taylor commented on how workers would need to "relearn" the ways they work to be compliant and more effective for their employers. He noted, "Each worker must learn how to give up his own particular ways of doing things, adapt his methods to the many new standards, and grow accustomed to receiving and obeying directions covering details, large and small,

Pen and ink drawing of Frederick Winslow Taylor by Robert Kastor, autographed December 5, 1913, with inscription, "A big day's work for a big day's pay." Taylor was a pioneer of scientific management, which workers detested and resisted. *Library of Congress, Prints and Photographs Division.*

which in the past have been left to his individual judgment. Supervisors would do the thinking for the workers."

Workers resisted. Almost all hated Taylor's principles. Taylor threatened lower wages, layoffs and fines. He might have understood motion studies, but Taylor did not understand human nature. When workers were let go, others were often uncomfortable replacing them. Workers did not want to stay at places that enforced such strict laws. In New York City garment shops and other manufacturing sites, scientific management as a complete methodology never caught on. However, its philosophy remained. Supervisors in manufacturing shops viewed their workers less as a set of individuals and more as an interchangeable set of workers to maximize output.

DIVISIONS WITHIN UNIONS

Workers were more determined than ever to fight for better conditions. By the late 1800s, a young leader, Samuel Gompers, emerged as a union leader. A former cigar maker, he stewarded the American Civil Labor

Union. This organization's goals were simple: higher wages and shorter hours. It fought for justice.

But unions were not always so unified. A big problem was the exclusion or inequality of Black and women members. Often, White male workers saw Black workers as a threat. They often worked for less pay and under worse conditions. The same prejudice applied to female workers. The American Federation of Labor (AFL), though, reasoned that Black men should be included in unions to avoid competition. In the 1880s, it issued a policy forbidding member unions to bar Black members. The approach was not an assertion of a philosophic moral statement. Rather, it was a practical stance to stave off unnecessary competition and to strengthen the federation through increased numbers.

As the nation's economic fortunes changed, so did the attitudes of union members towards Black people. To many members of the American Federation of Labor, Black members were "dangerous competitors, scabs who threatened white jobs and white unions."

Samuel Gompers echoed this sentiment. He observed, "Blacks had so conducted themselves to be a continuous convenient whip placed in

The Bakers and Big Loaf Parade in May 1909. Signs are held in Yiddish. Workers were celebrating their professions and fighting for more rights. *Courtesy of the Library of Congress, George Bain Collection Division of Prints and Photographs.*

the hands of the employers to cow the white men and to compel them to accept abject conditions of labor."[78] Gompers and other trade unionists also vehemently advocated for immigration restriction in the 1900s and 1910s. Their goal was to reduce the supply of labor to maintain wages and gain more bargaining leverage.

The AFL started to admit local unions that had excluded Black people. They were also largely excluded from skilled jobs. Sociologists like W.E.B. Du Bois lamented this riff but saw the union of Black and White people in the fight for improved labor conditions as inevitable. In 1907, he noted, "It is only a question of time when white working men and black working men will see their common cause against the aggressions of exploiting capitalists. The economic strength of the Negro cannot be beaten into weakness, and therefore it must be taken into partnership, and this the Southern white working man, befuddled by prejudice as he is, begins dimly to realize it."[79]

However, there were some positive alliances between White and Black workers in unions. For instance, the International Longshoremen's Union wanted to sidestep contending with Black stevedores, longshoremen and screwmen. So, the union accepted them as members. A good example of where White and Black dockworkers stood together was in New Orleans. "They agreed to share jobs half-and-half, the two races stood together in a notable strike in 1907. White employers who at first refused to even meet with black workers caved into the union's demands. It was an extraordinary moment—and a rare one too."[80]

Unions were often more opposed to having women in their unions than Black workers. Many skilled tradesmen believed they belonged in the home. Some male members held the misperception that women did not really need their earnings. They earned "pin money" for luxuries rather than for household necessities. Some men also believed that female workers accepted lower wages and therefore decreased the amount employers would pay. "It is the men who suffer through the women who are employed in the manufacturing of clothing. The girls can afford to work for small wages and care nothing about the conditions of the trade."[81] The AFL argued, "Every woman employed displaces a man and adds one more to an idle contingent that are fixing wages at the lowest limit." The union argued that there was circular logic. As women brought down men's wages, the households earned less so women had to then find more work, disrupting the home further.

Some wage-earning women had little interest in organizing because they were planning to work only until they were married. Such a plan was the norm during this period. Also, many were from countries with little to no tradition of labor organization.

The Women's Trade Union League (WTUL) tried to bridge these gaps. It was somewhat successful in New York. There were about 350,000 members at its peak. Nevertheless, the percentage of women in unions decreased from about 3.3 percent in 1900 to only about 1.5 percent in 1910.[82]

Some challenged the constitutionality of giving "special rights" or protections to women. However, courts were generally willing to let laws protecting women stand. Their reasoning was that women were weaker than men and, therefore, needed certain protections. "The employer and the laborer are practically on equal footing, but these observations do not apply to women and children," declared the Nebraska Supreme Court in 1902. Other state courts noted that a woman's reproductive health had societal implications and therefore should be protected. "Inherent differences between the two sexes—that woman's physical structure and the performance of maternal functions place her at a disadvantage in the struggle for existence is obvious. As healthy mothers are essential to vigorous offspring, the physical well-being of women becomes an object of public interest and care to preserve the strength and vigor of the race."[83] Notably, courts did not afford the same legal safeguards for men. The New York State

Woman on float of the Women's Auxiliary Typographical Union of a Labor Day Parade in New York in 1909. Labor Day was an important holiday at that time, celebrating workers' rights. *Library of Congress, Prints and Photographs Division.*

Photograph shows crowd at a labor sympathy parade in New York City on December 2, 1916. People hold signs reading "We demand the liberty of all the labor prisoners," "We demand justice for the Minnesota prisoners" and "Our brothers in Minnesota prison must be freed." Another sign is in Yiddish. *Library of Congress, Prints and Photographs Division.*

Legislature in Albany tried to limit the number of hours for bakers. But the Supreme Court struck it down, noting that men were "in no sense wards of the state. The government must not pass laws that were meddlesome interferences with the rights of the individual."[84]

These protections were a mixed blessing. On the one hand, they shielded women wage earners from exploitation, at least in theory. On the other hand, they created divides among all wage earners: "Male and female workers had less reason to recognize their common plight; male unionists had still less incentive to organize laboring women."[85]

Racial and gender differences were only part of the reason women and Black people tended to be excluded. Another was skill differential. Generally speaking, the AFL did not wish to unite skilled workers with the unskilled. As an example, when the United Brewery Workers tried to form an industrial union, the AFL expelled it in 1907. The AFL established industrial departments to manage craft unions in the same industry, like beer making, but the federation was loath to unify the skilled and less-skilled.[86]

ETHNICITIES

Managers of firms often played groups against each other to keep wages low and to keep unionization at bay. For example, the Progressive labor economist and University of Wisconsin at Madison professor John Commons observed the following phenomenon at a packing company in 1904:

> *I saw seated around the benches of the company's employment office a sturdy group of Nordics. I asked the employment agent, "How come you are employing only Swedes?" He answered, "Well, you see, it is only for this week. Last week we employed Slovaks. We change about among the different nationalities and languages. It prevents them from getting together. We have the thing systemized. We have a number of men in the field who keep us informed. If agitators are coming in or expected and there is considerable unrest among the labor population, we raise the wages all around. The unrest stops and the agitators leave. Then when things quiet down, we reduce the wages to where they were.*[87]

Most Americans were not members of unions. They had little negotiating power in wages, conditions and work performed. Work was mind-numbing, monotonous and dangerous. Scientific management exacerbated this tedium. Workers could be fired for forming unions. Federal, state and local laws were on the side of employers. During this period, socialism was on the rise in Europe and the United States. In New York, its membership grew. Newspapers like the *Forward* catered to this perspective. New York's Meyer London was a Socialist congressman.

In New York State, the public was lukewarm on unions. Some feared it was anti-American. Others were alarmed by the violence of strikes or questioned the motives of labor unions.

Labor strife would become more pronounced over the subsequent years. Various social labor groups were demanding more government action. Rejecting charity, which they said addressed only short-term needs, groups wanted public works programs to boost employment.

Working-class Americans were outraged that the city was not helping them. Before the Progressive Era, there were very few labor laws or social safety nets. High-income New Yorkers disapproved of the city helping the poor. The philosophy of rugged individualism persisted.

There were a few local events, however, that influenced New Yorkers' opinion favorably toward unions.

Tompkins Square Riots

To fight for worker protections, an umbrella group of unionists, socialists and labor reformers came together as the Committee for Safety. The group tried to secure a meeting with city officials. Their efforts were rebuffed. In response, the committee coordinated demonstrations in early January 1874 in Tompkins Square Park, located in the East Village. At the time, it was known as Klein Deutschland or "Little Germany" for its high concentration of German immigrants.

It was a spot familiar to many protestors from previous rallies and as a military parade ground during the Civil War. Many laborers of Irish and German descent who lived in the neighborhood planned to march to city hall and demand action. When the marchers reached city hall, police told them that they would not get to meet with city officials.

Around this time, a more militant demonstration was heating up, led by Patrick Dunn. This group encouraged protestors to use direct action if the government did not meet their demands. The relationship between the two protesting groups was uneasy. The Committee for Safety was wary of violence of any sort.

A crowd of over one thousand assembled on January 8 in Union Square. The police were ready in full gear. The Committee for Safety supporters convinced the crowd not to march to city hall, where a confrontation was likely. Instead, they suggested marching to Tompkins Square. The crowd voted for an eight-hour workday, as well as other demands. The remainder of that day passed without incident from the police. Participants were encouraged to return on January 13.

Despite the Committee for Safety's determination to keep the march peaceful, newspapers portrayed the movement as reckless and dangerous. They warned that the groups were armed with stolen weapons. On January 13, the police did not allow the group gathering at Tompkins Square to march to city hall but only to Union Square. The governor refused to intervene.

The group decided to scrap the march and convene at Tompkins Park, where they held a permit. However, the night before the meeting, the Department of Parks revoked the permit. Almost all protestors had no idea the permit was rescinded and showed up at Tompkins Park as planned. Over seven thousand turned up, making it among the largest demonstrations in New York City history at that time. Over sixteen hundred policemen stood on guard. Remarkably, there were no posters to inform participants that the permit had been revoked. By mid-morning, police stormed into the park and beat participants with clubs. Horseback police cleared the nearby streets. Confused, many fought back. One policeman was hit in the head with a hammer.

A young Samuel Gompers, who would eventually become a prominent labor leader, described the event:

> *By the time the first marchers entered the Square, New Yorkers were witnessing the largest labor demonstration ever held in the city. When the demonstrators had filled the square, they were attacked by the police.*
>
> *Mounted police charged the crowd on Eighth Street, riding them down and attacking men, women, and children without discrimination. Women and children went screaming in all directions. Many of them were trampled underfoot in the stampede for the gates. In the street, bystanders were ridden down and mercilessly clubbed by mounted officers.*
>
> *It was an orgy of brutality. I was caught in the crowd on the street and barely saved my head from being cracked by jumping down a cellarway.*[88]

Panic ensued across the city. Many residents claimed to have run away from protestors. In total, over forty-six arrests were made. Some served jail sentences of a few months. The governor eventually pardoned many.

The longer-term effect of the Tompkins Square riots on the labor movement in New York was negative. Much of the movement's momentum was lost. One example was the psychological impact on the young Samuel Gompers, who had witnessed the event. It convinced him that political radicalism did not achieve positive outcomes.

The Committee for Safety dissolved itself. Though some tried to indict police officers involved for their outrageous actions, little was done about it. Ironically, police harassment of political organizations increased during this period. Sometimes, police would justify their actions by inventing radical communist plots and then claiming that they must disrupt them.

TEXTILE MILL STRIKE

In 1912, workers at textile mills in Lawrence, Massachusetts, launched a fierce strike against very brutal working conditions. The strike would ultimately involve New York City in its information campaign. Wages were deplorable, as were the housing conditions for the textile mill workers. When the company announced a significant pay reduction, workers spontaneously went on strike. Strike leaders appealed to the International Workers of the World (IWW) for help.

Mill owners convinced the government to send in the militia to put down the strike. But the strike leaders devised an innovative publicity stunt to call attention to the plight of their workers. They put 120 children on a train bound for New York City. These children were greeted at Grand Central Station. Nurses who inspected them were appalled at the poor and ragged conditions of the workers' children. Public sympathy grew for the workers. Then, another group of children were sent to New York and were paraded up Fifth Avenue to draw more attention.

To counter the momentum for workers, a group of militias beat up the next group of children. But their efforts backfired. The public grew more outraged and demanded action from Congress, who agreed to hearings. At these hearings, young women told of the harrowing conditions in which they were forced to work. The mill owners eventually gave in and restored the wages.

GARMENT UNION STRIKES

By 1909, there was some progress in ameliorating conditions for workers in some industries—but not in clothing factories. The garment industry was fiercely competitive. Men, women and children toiled under inhumane conditions.

"You were locked into your space. If you were sick, you could be fired. You might be working a 16–20 hour day. You might be doing fine sewing without proper lighting. You were paid by the piece so speed was everything," explained a historian. Paychecks were docked for not making quotas. Doors were locked to keep out union organizers. Shop girls were fired for talking.[89]

Progressives trouped to Albany for changes. But they did not succeed. Tammany Hall stood in their way. Albany also would not budge. It was laissez-faire economics. The government allowed private businesses to do as they pleased. But the pressure was kept on the garment factories. By 1909, women showed up at Cooper Union. As the night wore on, leaders cautioned a general strike. Then, a weak worker who was beaten spoke to the crowd, saying, "I am a working girl. I am tired of listening to speakers who speak in general terms. I move that we go to a general strike." Her motion was endorsed. The next day, they joined the picket lines.

Pauline Newman, a textile worker, described her predicament: "Thousands left their factories and walked towards Union Square. It was November. The cold winter was just around the corner. We had no fur coats to keep us warm. And yet, there was the spirit that led us on and on." Tammany Hall broke up the strike. Many were arrested. The union's resources were consumed after a month or two. The uprising of twenty thousand started strong, but the bitter cold and dwindling resources took their toll. Three months later, more strikes ensued. But their success was limited. Many employers refused to sign any protocol agreement. The government did not enact any laws.

TRIANGLE SHIRTWAIST FIRE

More than any other labor event, a tragic incident near New York University on March 25, 1911, would forever change the way the public felt about worker rights and safety. It began as a typical day in the sweatshop in New York's Washington Square neighborhood. Immigrant workers were toiling away making ladies' garments called shirtwaists. The work was arduous, monotonous and strenuous. It was very low paying. Worse yet, the owners of the factory, Max Blanck and Isaac Harris, locked their workers in. That was, of course, a fire hazard. They did so, they said, to prevent workers from stealing. An unstated reason was also to keep out union organizers. Workers were often punished or fired for even mentioning the word *union*. The owners feared that if workers organized, they would gain too much power in demanding changes.

Around 4:45 p.m., just before closing, one of the great tragedies began to unfold. Probably from a cigarette or a haywire sewing machine, a fire broke out. The flames grew. Panicked, the workers ran toward the door to escape. But the door was locked. The owners had escaped through the rooftop, and they never unlocked the door.

The fire started to overtake the floor. Fire trucks arrived, but their ladders could not reach beyond the sixth floor. In the chaos, many jumped out of the window. Bystanders and firefighters watched helplessly from the streets. Sadly, there were corpses lining the roads.

A witness recounted in court documents: "I heard someone cry Fire. I ran for the door. But the door was locked. There was a great jam of girls. Some were screaming. Others were beating the door with their fists."

Some escaped safely. But soon after, the elevators started to break down. Hallway doors were locked. The fire escape gave way to the flames. The remaining women were trapped in the building with no means of escape. One witness heard a victim cry out goodbye in Italian.

Witnesses would later say the images they saw were seared in their memories for life.

One observer recounted, "Thud, dead. Thud, dead. Thud, dead. The first ten thuds shocked me. Then, I looked above and saw scores of girls."

Dozens of girls could be seen engulfed in flames. Some girls grabbed each other by the hand and jumped to their death. Workers poured out of nearby factories.

One witness recalled, "The floods of water from the fireman's hose were stained red from blood. I looked upon the heap of dead bodies, and I remembered these girls were shirtwaist makers. I remembered their great strike of last year in which these same girls demanded more sanitary conditions and more safety precautions in these shops. These dead bodies were the answer."

It was over in less than half an hour. Firefighters inspecting the floors the next day found dozens of burned bodies. Some were still huddled over machines. Inspectors found eleven engagement rings. In all, 146 had died in the city's greatest industrial disaster. A mass funeral was held for the unknown victims. The emotions of despair turned to anger. People demanded reforms so that no similar accident would occur.

A meeting was called at the Metropolitan Opera House by those "horrified men and women of the city." At the meeting, a "young cap maker stood at the edge of the great opera house stage and in a voice hardly raised, though it reached every person in that vast audience, arraigned society for regarding human life so cheaply."[90] As a result, worker conditions started to improve. Plus, serious discussions over minimum wages began.[91]

The owners were brought to court to find out if they were at fault. They hired a well-known defense attorney. The defense argued in court that the owners did not know that the door was locked at the time of the fire. Thus they were not responsible. Several survivors of the fire testified at the trial, but their knowledge of English was very limited. They gave their best account of what happened, but the defense lawyers asked them to rephrase their testimonies. They could not. So, the defense team argued that their statements were rehearsed and that they were told what to say.

Because of the defense team's legal skills and the prosecutor's inability to show that the owners knew the doors were locked, the jury acquitted the owners. They also were awarded a substantial sum from their fire insurance company. The owners reopened their factory nearby. Two years later, they

Following the tragic Triangle Shirtwaist Factory fire, one of the worst tragedies in New York's history, a procession of men on horseback in 1911 pass near the site of the fire at Washington Square. *Library of Congress, Prints and Photographs Division.*

were arrested for locking in employees, as when visiting it, fire inspectors saw the exit door blocked by rows of sewing machines.

Though very tragic, the event did promote more sympathy for workers' rights. After the Triangle Shirtwaist Factory tragedy, the public was more understanding of worker plights and so was the government. Federal, state and local governments stepped up safety standards and enforcement. Union leaders demanded more changes. Organizations like the International Ladies' Garment Workers Union won more concessions for their members in ensuing years.

From the ashes of the fire emerged one of the greatest transformations in U.S. history. It was a moment that the city could no longer turn a blind eye to the reality of the sweatshops. It was a turning point. Change depended on the New York State Legislature, which was run by Charles Murphy, known as "Silent Charlie," the leader of Tammany Hall. Murphy saw that the New York demographics and political dynamics were changing. No longer was gaining or forcing the Irish vote sufficient. Tammany Hall would need to compete with new voices from other immigrant groups, local politicians and settlement house workers. Murphy supported investigating the factories.

It took four long years. The Factory Committee took hearings from police officials, fire inspectors, health officials and labor leaders. It launched a statewide tour of factories, starting with New York City.

The resulting legislation affected many aspects of factory law. Plant owners would be required to provide enclosed staircases, ventilation, washrooms, fire sprinklers and adequate lighting. Dangerous machinery was outlawed. Children under the age of fourteen could not work in factories at all.

Business interests were outraged. But nothing could stop the campaign to use the power of the state to change people's lives. In the years to come, as the leaders of the Factory Commission moved into positions of power, reformers would gain more and more measures. Frances Perkins, the secretary of labor, would remark decades later that the "New Deal began on March 25, 1911."

Other trade groups protested as well. Some, like actors and theater workers, were white collar. They fought for fair working conditions in the theater and equitable pay. In some cases, they wanted to share in some of the profits enjoyed by theater owners and producers of box office hits.

Theatrical union labor parade, where actors and other theater workers asserted minimum wages and fair working conditions. *Library of Congress, Prints and Photographs Division.*

Laws Protecting Workers

After the Triangle Fire, the third-worst disaster in New York City history, the local, state and federal governments finally took action to protect workers. New York State created a Factory Investigating Commission to examine sanitation, safety, wages, hours, fire hazards and child labor in a variety of workplace settings, including homes, since many worked in small factories inside tenements. "During the first year of its work, the commission sent investigators to workplaces and held public hearings all over the state, hearing 222 witnesses, including factory workers, public officials, union leaders, and civic leaders. They produced 3,000 pages of testimony and drafted 15 bills, seven of which were defeated in 1912 due to Republican opposition, but passed in the following years."[92]

Thirty-six of the commission's recommendations became law between 1911 and 1914. They became known as the "golden age of remedial factory legislation." Examples of laws were:

- Mandatory registration of factories so fewer would operate in anonymity
- Requiring employers to perform fire drills
- Installing automatic sprinklers
- Prohibiting smoking in factories
- Reorganizing the labor department of New York State
- Limiting hours of labor for women in canneries
- Improving housing conditions in labor camps for factory workers
- Installing seats for women in factories
- Prohibiting children from working in dangerous occupations

Public Sympathy Grows

From these events, the public increasingly sympathized with union causes. Various groups united in helping workers. Political leaders, social gospel pastors, liberal economists and other Progressives joined efforts to improve conditions. They increasingly sympathized with the hard lives of working-class wage earners. In the 1900s, an increasing number of middle-class Americans realized that "factories were stealing the sense of pleasure and purpose from manual labor." They noted with regret the dying out of the "all-round craftsman who knew his craft as a whole and saw in each task which came to him, a challenge to his knowledge and capacity."[93]

Some companies were more sympathetic toward workers' rights. In Rochester, photography pioneer George Eastman's Kodak Company, for example, sought to help workers in 1910 by introducing a profit-sharing program for all employees. The company also promoted Florence McAnaney to lead the human resources department. McAnaney would become one of the first women executives at a major U.S. company.

Importantly, Progressives and labor unions had different goals and values. Progressives were advancing a moral and middle-class agenda. They hoped business interests and the workers would transcend their class differences. While they applauded efforts of workers to assert their rights, Progressives were also skeptical of some of the unions' methods. They felt some of the tactics were overly confrontational. Jane Addams of Chicago's Hull House Settlement, for instance, lauded the "ring of altruism" but cautioned that unions "use their power to frustrate the designs of the capitalist, to make trouble for corporations and the public. A movement cannot be accomplished by men who are held together merely because they are all smarting under a sense of injury and injustice."[94]

But labor union leaders tended to see this attitude as condescending or naïve. Their goal was action. They sought to draw the working class together (or at least the skilled White men) and set it apart from other classes. Workers tended to see Progressives as too passive. They said that though their concerns were discussed, these exchanges did not result in higher pay, shorter hours or improved conditions.

Despite these criticisms against them, Progressives fought for more protections for female workers. They advocated for the state to limit the hours and even the occupations of wage-earning women. Indeed, some states prohibited women from "serving liquor, laboring in mines, delivering messages, and grinding metals."[95] By 1900, many states legislated maximum hours for women workers, particularly in factory work. But some of these laws were struck down in court.

Thus for reformers during the Progressive Era, improving labor conditions was complex. Many were moved by events like the Triangle Shirtwaist Fire, which shined a light on the dangerous conditions for workers. They supported unions to assert worker rights. They also saw that unions themselves were discriminatory toward various groups. Others had leaders that were corrupt.

In the end, it was the increased public and legislator sympathy for workers that led congressional committees to document the dangerous labor conditions. That along with advocacy from union leaders, some ministers, settlement workers and some politicians led to changes in the law.

Changing the business landscape was not only about providing more worker protections. Many reformers, like Teddy Roosevelt, argued that monopolies and trusts that crowded out the competition and smaller players needed to be broken up.

11

Anti-Monopoly and Fair Competition

Another hallmark of the Progressive Era was the attempt to control big businesses from merging and cornering markets. During the depression of the early 1890s, many large firms were struggling. They were competing against each other and bringing down prices, sometimes below their marginal costs. As a result, they often couldn't cover their fixed costs.

Consequently, from 1897 until about 1904, many companies merged. During this period, known as the great merger movement, 1,800 companies turned into 157. Newly merged companies included National Biscuit and National Glass, as well as American Bicycle and American Brass. While merging was an acceptable business practice, many firms were gaming the system by secretly forming alliances to inflate prices, control suppliers and receive kickbacks.

Ominously, these consolidated firms controlled more than 40 percent of the market, giving them an unfair pricing advantage. They often elbowed out small businesses. One newspaper decried, "Big business could well lead to one of the greatest social and political upheavals that have been witnessed in modern history." In many industries, oligarchies proliferated. Their market size allowed them to raise prices, increase railroad rates and raw material goods costs, cut wages, demand higher productivity and manipulate freight charges.

Michael McGerr's *A Fierce Discontent* argues that there were five ways legislators and influencers reacted to this unprecedented economic power of consolidated corporations:

1. Do nothing. Much of the rich favored this hands-off or laissez-faire method.
2. Advocate socialism. By the early 20th century, some believed public ownership of capital, to a certain extent, was needed.
3. Pass anti-trust laws to encourage competition.
4. Legislate regulations. Writing or revising laws often entailed Congress creating commissions to monitor industries like the railroads to ensure they did not overcharge.
5. Impose a tax. The idea was to return some of the wealth to the community. In practice, though, the taxes were small and not disincentives.

Teddy Roosevelt was a strong proponent of breaking up monopolies and trusts. He believed in free enterprise but felt that a few firms were rigging the system. They were cornering their markets illegally, shoving out smaller players and squeezing suppliers and customers from the lack of fair competition. He condemned monopolies and companies gaming the system: "It is generally useless to try to prohibit all restraint on competition, and where it is not useless, it is generally hurtful."

Roosevelt had heard many of the rumors about illegal oil kickbacks to railroads. So, he ordered a federal investigation of Standard Oil. The report found that the company "has habitually received from the railroads, and now is receiving secret rates, and other unjust, illegal discriminations." It also showed that the company exercised "monopolistic control from the well of the producer to the doorstep of the consumer."[96]

At the center of the oil trust controversies was John Rockefeller. Lawmakers questioned whether his outsized influence and illegal kickbacks posed a threat to the nation's overall well-being. His Standard Oil Company had immense political influence. He bought out local refineries to drive up costs. He controlled about 90 percent of refining capacity. Many felt this dominant vertical integration gave the company tremendous unfair advantages over smaller or mid-sized producers. Regulators also accused the company of colluding with rival companies on prices and production limits. Moreover, the company was known for providing illegal kickbacks to partners, distributors or clients who gave an unfair advantage over its competitors.

Leading investigative journalist Ida Tarbell broke the controversy of this company. Her book *The History of the Standard Oil Company* exposed the underhanded and illegal practices of the dominant oil company. The daughter of an oil refiner driven out of business, Tarbell sought to show how bribes largely built dominant industry players. Tarbell was one of the muckraking journalists who exposed the dirt underneath storied institutions.

Cartoon shows two artists, President Woodrow Wilson and an overweight man labeled "Business Interests," painting portraits of Uncle Sam. Wilson's portrait shows Uncle Sam as robust and confident. The businessman's portrait shows him as frail and emaciated. In the winter of 1914, the New York economy was declining steeply. *Clifford Berryman, cartoonist, Library of Congress, Division of Prints and Photographs.*

The U.S. Justice Department filed a suit under the Sherman Act to dissolve Standard Oil Company. A federal court sided with the government in 1909. The court's decision withstood appeals, with the U.S. Supreme Court ruling in 1911 that Standard Oil Company must allow itself to be broken up. It was a landmark victory for the antitrust movement.

A fiery Teddy Roosevelt campaigns against monopolies in 1900. *Library of Congress, Prints and Photographs Division, NYWT&S Collection.*

At the time of this U.S. Supreme Court ruling, Teddy Roosevelt was out of office. On hearing the news on a safari trip in Africa, he exclaimed, "This is one of the most signal triumphs for decency which has been won in our country." His successor, William Taft, brought more antitrust suits, including pursuing justice against U.S. Steel.

While these efforts broke up some trusts and monopolies, they did not shake up the unfair competition as much as advocates had hoped. Congress's Clayton Act in 1914, for example, tried to establish tighter definitions of restraint of trade and harsher penalties for illegal trusts. But the act was filled with loopholes and seen as ineffective.

New Yorkers worried that monopolies impeded the interests of the republic. Americans feared their nation was becoming Europeanized. Europe had an aristocracy, income inequality and monarchies. Americans did not want the industrialists to become the new aristocracy. Americans felt opportunities for most were disappearing. Start-up costs for new businesses rose astronomically.

New Yorkers worried about the rise in extreme inequality. Notably, they were OK with some income inequality but not extreme inequality. The economic stratification data shows they had reason to be concerned. In 1890, the top 1 percent owned 51 percent of all wealth. The lowest 44 percent owned just 1.2 percent of all wealth. The top 12 percent controlled 86 percent of the wealth. Worse yet, big business was corrupting democracy. Politicians accepted bribes for favors to corporations. In New York State, Jay Gould's Erie Railroad and Vanderbilt's railroad bribed many in the New York State Legislature.

The political landscape was shifting. Emerging from a mindset of rugged individualism, the United States was starting to accept regulation as a necessary way of doing business. Legislators, the media and lobbyists began to view regulation as important for protecting consumers, keeping products safe and conserving the environment.

ROOSEVELT AND TRUST-BUSTING

Roosevelt believed everyone should have a chance to succeed. From a wealthy family, he believed that democracy and opportunity went hand in hand. So, he was alarmed when he saw the outsized influence of big corporations and Wall Street. He saw it as his mission to take on the biggest trusts. He started with the North Securities Trust. The judicial branch agreed, and the U.S. Supreme Court, in 1904, mandated that the trust put together by J.P. Morgan had to be broken up. Wall Street and Morgan were horrified. They had not expected a president to intervene.

The meatpacking industry was also plagued with corruption, and a few large companies controlled the market by stifling competition. Roosevelt and the U.S. Supreme Court broke that industry up as well.

He expounded, "The great corporations or trusts are the creatures of the State, and the State not only has the right to control them, but it is in duty bound to control them wherever the need of such control is shown."

For Roosevelt, there were good trusts and bad trusts. He left alone those trusts he felt were not harmful. He never offered a strict definition of the criteria for good versus bad trusts. He and his party were also unhappy with the size of banks and their ability to manipulate the stock market. His successor, William Taft, pursued antitrust measures more broadly, going after large industries like oil, tobacco and railroads.

Editorial cartoon shows Uncle Sam examining the teeth of a powerful horse offered by Senator Nelson W. Aldrich. *Artist Udo Keppler, Library of Congress, Prints and Photographs Division.*

TEDDY ROOSEVELT'S TRUST–BUSTING TESTED

During the Progressive Era, there were scares that gave rise to bank runs, particularly in New York City. In the fall of 1907, for example, copper prices collapsed. This fall raised fears about banks and trust companies that had lent heavily in the mining industry. On October 22, 1907, scared depositors made a run on the Knickerbocker Trust Company in New York City, which had deep business relationships with copper. The company was shut down the next day. Throughout Manhattan, terror spread. In the streets of New York, there were "men and women dashing about in the manner of ants when their hill is trodden on." Suddenly, many banks throughout New York could not meet their obligations. J.P. Morgan stepped in to calm the markets.

But the banks were still jittery. Roosevelt knew he had to step in. In trying to save the banks, he made a deal with the devil, which betrayed his deeply held antitrust beliefs. The Trust Company of America would have to be bailed out. The financial markets would need to infuse money, but this effort was limited by underwriters Moore and Schley. That firm needed to sell its shares in the Tennessee Coal and Iron Company. These transactions would prop up the stock market.

But who would purchase these shares? The deal became a double-edged sword for Roosevelt. U.S. Steel agreed to purchase these shares on the condition that the government would not pursue legal action on its acquisition of Tennessee Coal and Iron Company. Roosevelt agreed, but this gave U.S. Steel an unfair advantage in the southern market. Roosevelt was caught between saving the financial markets and his antitrust principles.

Consumer Protection

In policing business, reformers also looked at ways to protect consumers. Health advocates were concerned about preservatives and dyes used in food. Other watchdogs noticed that the drug industry was also misrepresenting itself. Snake oil salesmen were still selling "patented" potions in bottles as "cures" for a variety of ailments. In reality, these were often useless solutions that helped nothing, except the drug maker's bank account.

The media helped break many of these stories of deceptive consumer practices. In 1905, *Ladies' Home Journal* disclosed the fraudulent advertisements used to sell Lydia Pinkham's Vegetable Compound and other home remedies. Importantly, the public began to question product claims.

Perhaps the most famous novel from this period was Upton Sinclair's *The Jungle*. It described the desperate plight of meatpacking workers, many of whom were immigrants who toiled under perilous and burdensome conditions. It shined a spotlight on the unsanitary and flat-out dangerous ways meat was produced. It depicted meat "tainted by sawdust, human spit, and rat excrement." The book's sales soared from public curiosity, and "the sensational revelations of *The Jungle* appalled the public, infuriated meatpackers, and cut the sale of meat."[97]

Physicians, industry experts and women's groups supported legislation to protect consumers from tainted meat, drugs and foods. Some corporations supported this legislation, too, like beer maker Pabst and condiment producer H.J. Heinz, who sought stability in their markets and the restoration of public faith. They also saw regulation as increasing their producing costs, thereby raising the entry barriers for competitors.

The public's raised awareness of defective consumer goods also helped reformers push health care legislation. Dresses and cigars that were made in New York City's Lower East Side, for example, were said to have possibly contagious germs in them. After all, the factory workers might have had tuberculosis or an onslaught of other diseases. In other words, reformers made it the problem of customers that many of the workers behind the products they consumed toiled in unsafe conditions. This clever public relations move created an urgency for increased protections for both laborers and consumers.

The public perception of government was changing. From the founding of the nation to the 1870s, the general belief was that government should be small, with private enterprise unfettered. But in the late 1800s, a new notion emerged. The government came to be viewed as the protector of the power of the people—not the oppressor or impeder of liberty. It needed to protect consumers, workers and smaller producers. For some, it also needed to tax personal income, even if that necessitated the passage of a constitutional amendment.

12

PERSONAL INCOME TAX

Leveling the Playing Field

For the most part, the rich paid virtually no income taxes until the Progressive Era. By the 1890s, though, this staple of the Gilded Age and the decades before it was vanishing. The public started to support taxes on large incomes and inherited estates. For social reformers, taxing wealth would be a way to increase government revenues to spend on much needed public goods. For some, it was also an issue of fairness. Some believed it was unfair that business leaders and owners who made much of their fortune from societal goods would not then contribute to it in the form of taxes. Others saw the current system as perpetuating the wealthy class while shutting the door to anyone else.

The taxation issue exemplified many of reformers' goals during the Progressive Era. They sought to level the playing field—even if just a little—between the robber barons and other wealthy industrialists and the workers they employed. This philosophy, of course, stood in direct contrast to conservatives who believed that human nature is unchanging and operates on incentives and that the federal government should remain small in size and scope. They saw income tax as punishing those who produced capital and jobs. Moreover, conservatives saw taxes as a disincentive for opening new businesses and taking on risk. They feared it would put a drag on economic activity.

This national conflict played out in New York State. Some of the state's most influential politicians of the period generally supported some income tax. Most notable was President Theodore Roosevelt. He believed that taxing wealth was justified because, after all, part of that wealth was derived from using society's resources. He also objected to estates going un-taxed, because this system perpetuated the same families' status for subsequent generations without any benefit to the larger society from which this family has drawn resources. Roosevelt explained his position: "The man of great wealth owes a peculiar obligation to the State because he derives special advantages from the mere existence of government. Not only should he recognize this obligation in the way he leads his daily life and in the way he earns and spends his money, but it should be recognized by the way in which he pays for the protection the State gives him."

Breaking from his class, Andrew Carnegie argued the dire need for philanthropy and an inheritance tax. Though controversial and hotly debated, his article "Gospel of Wealth," written in 1889, inspired economists to rethink the distribution of wealth. He asked for the upper class to "utilize their surplus means in a responsible and thoughtful manner." He argued against upper-class overspending and self-indulgence. He cautioned that simply giving to a charity without addressing underlying root causes would prolong the current system rather than change it. Carnegie's ideas challenged notions of responsibility of upper classes.

The rich themselves were taken aback by what they saw as an intrusive income and inheritance tax. Very few joined Andrew Carnegie's call for giving away a significant sum of their wealth to worthy causes during their lifetime. One socialite commented, "I remember, even in my lifetime, a period when the people of this country looked up with admiration and respect to their wealthy classes."

Finally, Congress bowed to public pressure. The Sixteenth Amendment, allowing income tax, was ratified in 1913. Three years later, Congress "raised the income tax rates and enacted the first permanent inheritance tax, which included a maximum levy of 10% on estates over $5 million."

This legislation showed that the working and middle classes exerted political power despite the relatively small proportion of the wealth they held. It also exposed a change in public opinion about the wealthy. Perhaps as a result of Progressive activist protests and calls for reform, middle and working-class people realized that the rich should be contributing fairly. Andrew Carnegie's speeches agreeing with these taxes lent more credibility to the issue.

However, for most politicians, what spurred the passage of this constitutional amendment was the proposal of Prohibition. Knowing that if the purchase and sale of alcohol was made illegal, governments

History of Personal Income Tax

Personal taxation had been occurring since colonial times. However, it was in a regional and limited way. Some southern states had enacted taxes on income from the property before and after the War for Independence (1776–83). The U.S. Constitution allowed the national government to increase taxes at a uniform rate and stipulated that "direct taxes be imposed only in proportion to the census population of each state."

The outbreak of the Civil War brought personal taxation to the forefront. Congress introduced the Revenue Act of 1862, a national income tax, to defray war costs. This legislation "imposed a 3% tax on incomes of citizens earning more than $600 per year and 5% on those making over $10,000."* This act expired in 1872, and the government relied on tariffs and excise tax for the majority of its revenue. Congress initiated a limited graduated tax in 1894.

But the tax was legally challenged in *Pollock v. Farmers' Loan & Trust Company*. In this case, Charles Pollock sued the corporation he owned stock in, alleging that the company erred by paying an unconstitutional income tax. The legal reasoning was that the Constitution allowed only for the tax that was apportioned by population. The courts focused on the exact language in the Constitution in Article I, Section 9, Clause 1, which notes, "All Duties, Imposts and Excises shall be uniform throughout the United States" and "no Capitation, or other direct, Tax shall be laid, unless in Proportion to the Census or Enumeration herein before directed to be taken."

Therefore, the Constitution mandated direct taxes based on a census. For example, if the federal government hypothetically needed to net $50 million per year and New York State comprised 15 percent of the total U.S. population, New York State residents would need to raise $7.5 million. If New York State had one million residents, each would need to pay $7.50. The logic was that no individual unduly carried the tax burden.

Consequently, the U.S. Supreme Court found the tax unconstitutional in *Pollock v. Farmers' Loan & Trust Company* in a 5-4 decision. The court objected to "direct taxation" that was "not apportioned among states as required by the constitution." Thus, the 1894 tax law was ruled unconstitutional and was effectively repealed.

---

* Constitutional Rights Foundation, "The Income Tax Amendment: Most Thought It Was a Great Idea in 1913," crf-usa.org.

would drastically suffer from a loss of excise tax. Enacting a personal and inheritance income tax would compensate for much of these losses. Thus the passage was based more on economic practicality than on notions of social justice. Still, its passage was a win for social reformers.

MIXED REACTION TO AMENDMENT

To advocates of personal and inheritance tax, it was clear that the only viable path was to change the Constitution through an amendment. By 1909, many Americans agreed with the passage of an income tax on individuals and corporations.

As summarized above, Congress passed the amendment on July 2, 1909. Four years later, the requisite number of states ratified it. Finally, on February 25, 1913, it was certified as part of the U.S. Constitution. Sweeping tax reforms followed with the passage of the Sixteenth Amendment. First, Congress allowed for excise taxes at 1 percent of each corporation's income over $5,000. Additionally, the Sixteenth Amendment allowed for Congress to "have the power to lay and collect taxes on incomes, from whatever source derived, without apportionment among the several States, and without regard to any census or enumeration."

Various parts of the political spectrum drove its support. Agricultural communities in the Midwest and South loathed tariffs, which they feared might be imposed if the personal income tax was not passed. They believed, rightly so, that tariffs increased prices and decreased demand for their products. Therefore, they were relieved to see income tax replace some of these oppressive tariffs. Reformers in the industrialized urban Northeast supported taxation. Some conservatives also supported it to offset losses in the excise tax, should Prohibition be passed, which many supported. Also, many conservatives saw a rising military threat from Japan, Germany and certain European nations. For that reason, they agreed with taxing to boost defense expenditures.

For reformers, it was a big win. They predicted the government would have more revenues to help disenfranchised citizens, including the poor and sick. They saw the amendment's passage as a great leveler. The working class and middle class in New York State generally favored the passage, with resistance from some but not all of the upper class. The latter was particularly concerned about their inheritance becoming overtaxed.

POLLY'S CHANCE TO GET SOME NICE CRACKERS.

"We don't want an Income-Tax Amendment! Say it, Polly! We don't want an Income-Tax Amendment! Say it, Polly! Amendment! Amendment! We don't want it!"

A well-dressed man labeled "Plutocracy," holding a parrot labeled "State Legislature" on his right hand. He is trying to get the parrot to repeat, "We don't want an Income-Tax Amendment!" and promising it "some nice crackers" in return for correctly learning to repeat the phrase. *Udo Keppler, Library of Congress, Prints and Photographs Division.*

This passage of the personal income tax coupled with antitrust measures and government protections for workers signaled a shift in how Americans viewed freedom. Since the nation's founding, freedom tended to mean "freedom from." That was often construed as liberty from an oppressive government or unfair taxation. Many Americans, of course, did not enjoy these liberties. During the Progressive Era, though, freedom came to mean the right to enjoy a certain quality of life. Thus, freedom seemed to mean "freedom from misery." Part of this newfound freedom would mean rooting out rampant government corruption.

NEW YORK STATE AND NEW YORK CITY PERSONAL INCOME TAX

Excise taxes on alcohol stopped with Prohibition, leaving a huge hole in New York State's budget. This shortage was compounded by slowdowns in manufacturing after World War I that decreased state corporate taxes. State lawmakers were in a bind. They knew their constituency would oppose a state income tax, but they saw no alternative. In 1919, the 142nd annual session of the legislature finally brought this change. Legislative leaders met with mayors in Albany to discuss the income tax passage. Republican assembly speaker Thaddeus Sweet of Oswego (near Syracuse) noted, "The only question to be decided is the rate to be fixed and what size incomes should be exempted."

"The state and localities will be deprived before the expiration of the coming year of several millions of dollars of revenue heretofore derived from liquor taxes," the state tax commission wrote in a February report. "We believe that the time has come to enter upon a more scientific method of raising revenues for State and locality and for the relief of real estate. In this connection, the Commission recommends the enactment of a general personal income tax at a low rate."

Farmers in upstate New York were particularly resistant to the idea. Representatives put forth alternative revenue sources, like a motor vehicle tax and soft drink fees. In the end, though, the state legislature passed the new tax code with little opposition: in the state senate 37-9 and in the assembly 140-0.

Significantly, the state income tax affected only high wage earners. The new tax called for a 1 percent surcharge on those earning $1,000 to $2,000 and 3 percent for the few who made more than $50,000. It's estimated that about five hundred thousand of the state's ten million people, about 5 percent, would owe taxes. Later, a far greater percentage of the state's working population would pay state income taxes.

In 1934, New York City became the first city to pass an income tax ordinance. But lawmakers withdrew the bill. Over the subsequent decades, many local municipalities passed a local income tax law. In 1966, New York City's newly inaugurated mayor John Lindsay adopted a local income tax that residents paid on top of their sales tax. Historians see the steep decline of New York City from the mid- to late 1960s until the early 1980s. One contributing factor to the city's decline could have been more affluent residents fleeing the city to avoid paying local income taxes and other urban issues.

Part VI

THE UNLIKELY ALLIANCE: SOCIAL REFORMERS AND MINISTERS

13

Cleaning up Corruption in New York

Decades Before Progressive Era—Pervasive Corruption

As the nation expanded after the Civil War's tumultuous end, new ideas and advancing technology created great wealth. With steel, oil, the telegraph and other tools, the city progressed markedly. New York City's industrial might exploded. It became the center of global finance. It also became a hotbed of corruption by businessmen, politicians, legislators and financiers.

No rules governed Wall Street. Consequently, many tried to rig markets or corner supplies of gold or silver. Embezzlement, kickbacks and illegal cornering of markets plagued the economy.

Ground zero for corruption in New York was an unfinished courthouse that stood near the Brooklyn Bridge that was still unfinished after twelve years of construction. It was started around 1860. Construction costs were skyrocketing as they lined developers' pockets. The courthouse became a symbol of the rampant corruption of the political machine Tammany Hall.

It was said that the men who ran Tammany Hall had no ideals, no platform and no morals. The statement was true, but it omits that some constituents liked Tammany Hall for addressing their immediate needs and giving them a voice and comfort. As a prime example, Tammany Hall reached out to the largely ignored and disliked Irish immigrants. Tammany Hall officials provided temporary food and shelter to many living in the notorious Five Points and the Lower East Side. They also

A poster depicting efforts to help the poor and clean up corruption of Mayor Seth Low versus the swindling behavior of Tammany Hall. However, a Tammany Hall candidate defeated Seth Low for mayor for a second term. *Metropolitan Lith. Studio Photograph, Library of Congress, Division of Prints and Photographs.*

assisted other immigrant groups, like Germans, eastern Europeans and Jews. Those looking for housing or a job would go to Tammany Hall for help. In return, of course, Tammany Hall expected—or forced—votes to keep them in office.

Tammany Hall was a corrupt political machine. But the organization privately saw itself as helping its constituents directly. If a family needed coal, for example, Tammany Hall would offer it to them rather than have them undergo a bureaucratic procedure with an uncertain response. A New York state senator explained this approach: "I don't ask whether they are Republicans or Democrats, and I don't refer them to the Charitable Organization Society, which would investigate their case in a month or two and decide they were worthy of help about the time they are dead from starvation. I get living quarters for them, buy clothes for them."[98] It was partly for this reason that despite its pervasive corruption, the party machine prevailed even against mayoral candidates seeking to clean up corruption. One example was Mayor Seth Low's defeat for reelection by a Tammany Hall candidate.

Boss Tweed

William "Boss" Tweed was an ex-firefighter before becoming the leader of Tammany Hall in 1858. Before the Progressive Era, he became the personification of corruption and government official abuses. Over six feet tall and three hundred pounds, he was said to be graceful on his feet. He was a consummate politician providing services for his constituents. He saw the power of mass politics in the city.

Tweed became part of the notorious Forty Thieves, a group of New York City aldermen who were known as the most corrupt politicians in the city's history. He was appointed to a supervisory board, which he saw as an opportunity for large-scale thievery. One common method was that the supervisory board would force vendors to pay a 15 percent surcharge as their ticket for conducting business in New York. It was open blackmail.

Tweed and his associates audaciously siphoned off large kickbacks from major building projects throughout the city. They pocketed, in today's dollars, hundreds of millions of dollars. By 1870, Tweed had concentrated more power in himself than any other previous politician had. In 1870, reformers and journalists began questioning where Tweed's lavish lifestyle had come from.

Construction on the New York County Courthouse, mentioned earlier, was supposed to cost $350,000. Twelve years later, the price tag reached $13 million. New Yorkers knew something had to be done. The upper classes had spoken despairingly of Tammany Hall and its corruption. Ultimately, they looked away, as its construction projects catapulted the real estate market. Tweed became the villain. Importantly, though often overlooked, he was not the only corrupt official. Bankers, lawyers, builders, city officials and law enforcement were all complicit. Tweed was corruption's visible face.

In December 1871, Boss Tweed was indicted on three counts of fraud and grand larceny. A judge ultimately sentenced him to prison. These convictions were later overturned. However, that didn't seem to matter, as Tweed was ailing in prison and spent his final years there. In 1878, he died in a cell in a Ludlow Street jail on the Lower East Side. His cell was just a few blocks from where he grew up on Cherry Street. He was penniless and broken. The poor, though, saw him as a friend to the needy. They saw his downfall as the "malice revenge of the wealthy."

REVEREND PARKHURST'S CRUSADE

Fed up with corruption and what they saw as personal vices proliferating, some Protestant ministers focused on improving the city. A key example was the Reverend Charles Parkhurst. He led the Madison Square Presbyterian Church near Twenty-Fourth Street and Fifth Avenue, where he demanded changes. In February 1892, he called out the corruption of "Tammany men ruling New York, especially the mayor, district attorney, and the police captains…a lying, perjured, a rum-soaked and libidinous lot." He accused them of licensing crime and looting the city for their financial gain.

Few outside of his congregation had heard of Parkhurst until that point. He noted that he was taking action not as a Democrat or as a Republican but as a Christian. He reminded congregants that the word *protestant* derived from the word *protest*. With that, he promised swift action.

Ministers like Parkhurst received scant public support in their efforts to root out local corruption. He also underestimated Tammany Hall's ability to fight back through law enforcement and the media. They charged him with libel and spreading vicious, unfounded rumors about them.

He did not anticipate the backlash. The district attorney called him before a grand jury on libel charges. The grand jury agreed that he attacked Tammany Hall unfairly. It noted that he "had no evidence on which to base his statements."

Parkhurst realized he needed to collect his own evidence. He decided to hire private detective Charles Gardner to take him on a "sin tour" of New York City. The tour showcased the underside of New York City during the Progressive Era. The two visited the so-called seedy side. They explored sailor dance halls and saloon boardinghouses catering to homesick sailors from different countries. Among the many places they visited was Jensen's. It was said that the clientele were mostly "sailors, thieves, pimps, shoestring gamblers, and the women, if they were in that joint, were 'abandoned.'"

They visited Chinese opium dens in Chinatown and hotels housing often drunk patrons. They also called on Little Italy, which was notorious for crime and violence. They saw a "stale beer" dive, which was considered the lowest type of saloon. The description portrays its roughness: "Dirt floor, a dark open underground rectangle with crude benches on the side, a plank for a bar. Unwashed tramps and derelict women clustered around kerosene lamps swilling ungodly brew from tomato cans. A fight broke between two missing-toothed women competing to be treated by Parkhurst's party."[99]

Parkhurst submitted his findings to the district attorney against hundreds of brothels, gambling joints and law-breaking saloons. Under pressure, the district attorney brought up charges. But the police paid off by Tammany Hall were suspicious of Parkhurst and his group investigating gambling joints and prostitutes on their beats. So, they set a trap for Parkhurst and his detective and "sin city" tour guide Charles Gardner. It was a sting operation, where Gardner was caught taking bribes and blackmailing. He was set up by one of the brothels he was trying to expose. Gardner's subsequent arrest was featured in headlines across city papers.

The tables turned. Gardner had set out to expose the illegal vices in the city for his employer Parkhurst. In the end, though, Tammany Hall—in an effort to protect its system—took down Gardner. Reverend Parkhurst tried defending Gardner, saying, "If the police would only show as much interest and eagerness to suppress evil as they do to suppress the efforts of our Society, there would be no cause for complaint."

Gardner's defense was of no consequence. At trial, a jury returned a guilty verdict against Gardner in a few hours. The *New York Times* agreed with the decision, calling Gardner the "vilest" of all men. It proclaimed, "These creatures will work, as Gardner did, for their own profit, and will sell out their employers and their causes without scruple."[100]

The Tammany Hall–backed police chiefs who instigated the sting on Gardner were rewarded. Bosses transferred them to lucrative beats where corruption and payoffs ruled supreme.

POLICE PAYOFFS

The Parkhurst case illustrates how pervasive corruption, bribes and payoffs were among the police as well as other public officials, including politicians and judges. Top police made huge fortunes from payoffs. Thomas Byrnes, one of the best known, had an estimated net worth of $350,000 (about $10 million in present dollars), even though as a public employee he had earned only around $5,000 annually. Byrnes had not been in any other official business than the police force.

Byrnes was later accused of accepting bribes, racketeering and more. When questioned in a court about how he made so much money as a public employee, he tried to explain it away by saying he had met some wealthy men who "from time to time helped me to make money."

Another police officer, Alexander "Clubber" Williams, also greatly profited from policing the most lucrative district—the Tenderloin. *Harper's* magazine considered him "the most venomously hated, frequently tried and most valuable of police officers." According to some anecdotes, "during his first days as a patrolman assigned to the corner of Broadway and Houston Street, he asked around to learn who were the toughest gang members in the neighborhood. He threw one, then the other through a plate-glass window."[101]

Supposedly on a policeman's salary, Williams owned a building on East Tenth Street, a large estate in Cos Cob, Connecticut, and a steam yacht named *Eleanor*.

CLEANING UP THE NEW YORK CITY POLICE FORCE

Nearly everyone recognized the need for great reform of the police force. It took on a national significance. "Editorial writers from Maine to California called for reform of the police in the nation's largest city. New York's *Finest* was accused of being New York's *Filthiest*. They ruled New York's street corners as an established caste with powers and privileges away above and beyond the people."[102]

By 1895, the scene had changed, with the appointment of a new police commissioner, Theodore Roosevelt. Seeing the enormous nepotism and hiring by political favors, Roosevelt and others insisted on civil service exams to hire for many city posts. Test scores would be an objective standard of hiring.

Unsurprisingly, the party bosses fought against civil service. They saw it as disconnecting citizens from their government. "How are you goin' to interest our young men in their country if you have no offices to give them when they work for their party," asked George Washington Plunkitt, a New York state senator and Tammany Hall official. "Isn't it enough to make a man sour on his country when he wants to serve it and won't be allowed unless he answers a lot of fool questions about the number of cubic inches of water in the Atlantic and quality of sand in the Sahara?"[103]

Roosevelt also hired a woman to work at the New York City Police Department, a controversial decision at the time. Roosevelt was gearing to clean up the police force. He would fire the corrupt, hire replacements and bring order to it. His ally Jacob Riis, a muckraking journalist for the *New York Tribune* among other newspapers, commented, "Teddy Roosevelt brought a moral purpose to the police force for the first time. The ordinary attitude toward a new commissioner is one of good-natured, half indulgent, half-amused deference. The coming of Roosevelt has made a sudden and extraordinary change."

Others were skeptical of his changes. New York journalist Lincoln Steffens, known for his article series in *McClure's*, observed, "The police were excited but could not believe it all at once. They laughed, they are cynics of the worst sort. They are confidently wicked. They have practiced corruption for so long that they believe it is good. They know it is—for it pays."[104]

Roosevelt instituted new hiring practices for policemen. He insisted on high moral character and passing a civil service written test that would be "simple, practical, and common sense." He also wanted his police to be more polite. He wrote, "We are bound to make all honest, brave, and efficient members of the force who are bold in their dealings with the criminals and courteous in their dealings with the ordinary citizens, understand that we are their friends."[105]

Direct Election of U.S. Senators

Another way corruption was rooted out in New York during the Progressive Era was through the passage of a constitutional amendment for direct election of U.S. senators. Throughout the country's history, state legislatures had chosen senators. For corruption-plagued New York State, senator selections were usually brokered by backroom deals, possible kickbacks or quid pro quo favors, and there was no transparency in the state legislature in Albany. The cycles of corruption perpetuated. With the direct voting of U.S. senators, though, the legislators were more accountable to voters of their state (which, in practice, was largely White males older than twenty-one).

Most likely, the founding fathers of the United States set up state legislatures to choose senators to balance state versus federal interests and to limit popular representation. The signers of the Constitution were careful to put in safeguards against a whimsical public. So, they balanced the U.S. House of Representatives, elected by popular vote, with the state legislature–appointed Senate. In retrospect, the signers of the Constitution might have over-controlled for popular support and underestimated how that system encouraged intra-government corruption.

In practice, though, many states held direct primaries for Senate races starting around 1890: "Between 1890 and 1905, thirty-one state legislatures passed resolutions either calling on Congress to pass an amendment providing for the direct election of senators, to hold a conference with other states to work on such an amendment, or to have a constitutional convention such that the direct elections for Senator could be included in a newly drawn Constitution."[106] Progressives sought to free the Senate from the influence of the corrupt state legislatures and lobbyists. They also pushed for referendums, nonpartisan elections and other constitutional changes at all levels of government.[107]

To spark the debate on the pending amendment, William Randolph Hearst hired muckraking journalist David Phillips to write an exposé series called *The Treason of the State.* The piece explained that direct senatorial elections would weaken the influence of large corporations and bring government "closer to the people." The articles were very popular with readers and significantly increased *Cosmopolitan*'s circulation. Others found the pieces grandstanding and muckraking.

In 1906, a federal court convicted two senators on charges of taking fees for interceding with federal agencies. This discovery reinforced the notion that senators who were chosen not by the electorate but by the state legislature were more likely to be corrupt. Congress and the requisite number of state legislatures ratified the Seventeenth Amendment in 1913. New York reformers hoped that would usher in a more accountable government.

Reformers turned their attention to changing individuals' consumption habits and vices. Interfering in people's lives, though, would ultimately prove to overstretch their agenda.

A Nation of Drunkards

In the nineteenth century, alcohol permeated most aspects of life. People would drink early in the morning and late into the night. Physicians advised their patients to drink beer instead of water, as water was often from unsanitary sources. Alcohol consumption was as American as apple pie. The *Mayflower* bringing over pilgrims in the seventeenth century contained cases of beer. A century later, George Washington made sure his men had enough rum or gin during major battles.[108] By 1830, the "average American over 15 years old consumed nearly seven gallons of pure alcohol a year—three times as much as we drink today—and alcohol abuse was wreaking havoc on the lives of many, particularly in an age when women had few legal rights and were utterly dependent on their husbands for sustenance and support."[109]

New York City was no exception. Some called the city a "beery paradise." There appeared to be a saloon or bar in every square inch of the bustling metropolis. As an illustration, an 1883 map of a "32-block section of the Lower East Side reportedly shows 242 large beer saloons and sixty-one liquor saloons. In the neighborhood to the north, there were 181 beer bars and seventy-six liquor establishments."[110] With the onslaught of German immigrants in the early to mid-nineteenth century, the number of saloons and beer gardens had multiplied dramatically.

With the preponderance of beer halls and bars, reformers watched as life savings were swallowed up and wives and children were abused due to one reason—alcohol. Americans would argue furiously over what to do about drunkenness. Hanging in the balance was a prohibition on alcohol, a decision

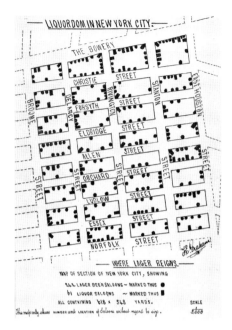

Map of saloons in New York City's Lower East Side. Anti-saloon activists strove to show a connection between a proliferation of saloons and crime. *Wikimedia Commons.*

that would turn millions of law-abiding citizens into lawbreakers. It would expose a divide of countryside and cities, as well as with natives and immigrants. The issue of alcohol consumption would raise questions about individual responsibilities and the defining of who was a "real American."[111]

For many, the United States had become a "nation of drunkards." They deplored what they believed was alcohol's corrupting influence on man. They felt strongly that the drunkards' families were victims. These reformers named their call for change the temperance movement. Initially, it was about moderation. Later, though, it demanded complete abandonment of alcohol. They reasoned that some needed help to overcome temptations, and only by making something illegal would that happen. Otherwise, people would not have the strength to resist alcohol.

In New York City, immigrants from Ireland, Italy, Germany, Poland, Greece and eastern Europe drank as a part of celebrations, family rituals and rejoicing. Going to a saloon was an escape. It was a comradeship among men and a refuge from a life of stress. The city's water was mostly undrinkable, and milk was often spoiled. Therefore, beer was the drink of choice for many New Yorkers. Saloons were omnipresent in many neighborhoods. For many New Yorkers, that prevalence was a positive attribute. But critics charged that alcohol's proliferation was tearing apart families and the moral fabric of society.

Questions arose about how immigrants in New York, and elsewhere, should behave. Just because they drank a lot in their home countries, did that mean they should behave the same in their new homeland? Were certain groups drinking the "wrong" alcohol? Reformers and pastors asked these often racially and ethnically tinged questions of themselves. But few asked the immigrant groups what they wanted.[112]

Some residents—often women or children—were intimidated by the saloons. One observer in Hell's Kitchen observed, "Men would be paid on Saturday afternoon, coming home drunken and abusive and the mother and children wondered how they'd get by. Women would cross streets to avoid passing by a saloon."[113]

RISE OF THE TEMPERANCE MOVEMENT

Temperance began as a movement in the 1830s and 1840s as a way to "cleanse the nation's soul." Some abolitionists opposed alcohol consumption, too. The temperance movement, "rooted in America's Protestant churches, first urged moderation, then encouraged drinkers to help each other to resist temptation, and ultimately demanded that local, state, and national governments prohibit alcohol outright."[114]

By the late nineteenth century, during the Progressive Era, women reformers were determined to put a stop to alcohol sales and purchases and to close bars across the United States:

> *After the Civil War, as millions of immigrants—mostly from Ireland, Germany, Italy, and other European countries—crowded into the nation's burgeoning cities, they worked hard to assimilate while simultaneously retaining cherished habits and customs from their homelands. The brewing business boomed as German-American entrepreneurs scaled up production to provide the new immigrants with millions of gallons of beer. In the 1870s, inspired by the rising indignation of Methodist and Baptist clergymen, and by distraught wives and mothers whose lives had been ruined by the excesses of the saloon, thousands of women began to protest and organize politically for the cause of temperance.*[115]

The organization came to be called the Women's Christian Temperance Union (WCTU). The WCTU wrestled state and federal legislatures for a "scientific temperance instruction" in schools. Importantly, the group focused on closing down saloons but not banning alcohol per se. To this group, the saloon was a hotbed of immoral behavior. By shutting down saloons, they believed they could improve communities. Initially, the organization advocated for allowing local jurisdictions to decide whether or not to close their saloons. American educator and indomitable suffragette Frances Willard of Evanston, Illinois, became its leader.

The WCTU was action oriented and very provocative by the standards of the day. The organization urged women to take to the streets to put the alcohol industry out of business. In towns and cities across the United States, they preached from portable tabernacles. Though support in New York City for the WCTU was tepid, it was substantial enough that Willard gave a speech there.

To win more support among women, Willard and other leaders of the temperance movement allied with the more established women's suffrage movement. Reformers called for "ballots as protection from the tyranny of drink." To win over women reticent to support the movement, Willard promoted the term "home protection," tying abolishing drinking to a woman's instinct to keep her family safe.

The WCTU and regional organizations with similar aims directed their chapters to pressure local school boards to teach the importance of temperance in classes. The educational content was largely propagandistic. It aimed to scare rather than impart verified information. Some were graphic and exaggerated, like the claim that one drink could "burn against the kidneys." Other assertions were ludicrous and lacked scientific backing, like the misstatement that alcohol could cause deafness or lunacy.

The anti-alcohol movement fit in with a larger list of Progressive Era concerns. The WCTU saw alcohol as the "underlying source of a long list of social ills and found common cause with Progressives trying to ameliorate the living conditions of immigrants crowded into squalid slums, protect the rights of young children working in mills and factories, improve public education, and secure women's rights."[116]

But the temperance movement in New York had mixed success. Immigrants who worked in laborious and often dangerous jobs in New York City resented being lectured to about how they chose to spend their leisure time and dollars. If they overspent the family budget, that was their business. For many, the saloons were a place to let loose.

Robert Graham was a visiting member of the Church of England Temperance Society, which sought to arouse anti-alcohol sentiments. In 1891, he preached the vices of alcoholism with mixed success. With a police escort, he toured some of New York City's most squalid slums. He documented his observations in a pamphlet called *Liquordom*. It contained maps of beer gardens, saloons and other alcohol-serving establishments. Like many Progressive reformers of his day, he strove to provide data to advance his argument. His pamphlet read, "On average, there was one saloon to every twenty-five families in the city; that 63 percent of all the criminal arrests were for intoxication and disorderly conduct; and that while the total number of food sellers—butchers, bakers, and grocers—was 7,197, the number of liquor sellers was 10,075."[117]

Graham was further troubled by what he saw as an intractable corrupt intertwining of local government and taverns. He lamented that twelve of the twenty-four aldermen of New York City were liquor dealers. He was highly concerned that election meetings were in or near establishments serving alcohol.

He cautioned, "The inferences to be drawn from the schedule are plainly that the saloon is master of the position; that the saloon-keepers are the political wire-pullers; that politicians, in the best sense of the term, do not care to submit to the thralldom involved in hobnobbing with keepers of corner groggeries; and that we have, therefore, the worst and not the best stratum from which to draw our municipal councilors and state legislators."[118]

Graham's pamphlet visually mapped out the preponderance of saloons. He also drew a link between neighborhoods with a high number of liquor-serving establishments and poverty. His writing was stark and dramatic. It sought to draw the attention of New York's religious leaders, social reformers, politicians and housewives. He described how the proliferation of saloons caused unsanitary conditions that deprived families of proper homes:

> *It is an undoubted fact that just where poverty and misery are greatest, there is the largest number of saloons. Granted squalid and overcrowded homes, with a minimum of comfort and a maximum of filth, it is not to be wondered at that saloons with polished woods, meretricious gilding, light, warmth, and freedom, should compete with and beat out of the field the three bare and comfortless rooms which are home only in name. To the real home in the city of New York, which is within the reach of every man in it, there can be no deadlier enemy than the 10,168 saloons which crowd its alleys and throng its courts.*[119]

William Henry Blair, a Republican senator from New Hampshire, echoed many of Graham's observations and sentiments. Blair was also a staunch supporter of Prohibition. He introduced the first bill in Congress to "ban the manufacture, sale, and distribution of alcoholic beverage." As did Graham in his book, William Blair's book, *The Temperance Movement or the Conflict between Man and Alcohol*, employed maps of saloons in New York City. He sought to show that neighborhoods with a high preponderance of saloons were less prosperous. He quoted Graham's observation that where there is poverty and misery in New York City, there is also the greatest number of saloons. However, neither Graham's nor Blair's books established causality. They showed that a high number of saloons *correlated* with but did not necessarily *cause* more poverty. In reality, other factors might have been causing these neighborhoods' impoverishment.

Blair's book chides the temperance movement for its overly measured response to saloons. He describes the half-baked efforts as "impotent." He called for full Prohibition by proclaiming, "The saloon is without a doubt the great visible factor of danger in our government. The anti-saloon movement is an effort to destroy it with any and every kind of available weapon, and to utilize the activity everybody who will even wish death to the saloon, although they will only pelt the rude boy in the apple tree with tufts of grass, hoping in due time the impotency of such warfare may induce them to throw the stones of total prohibition."[120]

Social Class and Prohibition

Liberal Progressives and Protestant ministers forged an unlikely alliance. Both groups saw the transformation of the individual and the importance of the home and family as the staple in society. First on their list was the abolition of alcohol. One Presbyterian minister lamented that alcohol was "the open sore of this land….The most fiendish, corrupt and hell-soaked institution that ever crawled out of the eternal pit." They objected to alcohol spurring illegal prostitution.

Moreover, reformers heard countless stories of alcoholic husbands beating their wives or children. In other households, fathers would "drink away" their paychecks shortly after receiving them. This negligence left their families in a constant cycle of poverty. Their efforts to prohibit alcohol in the 1890s met with success only in Kansas, Maine and North Dakota.

This triad crusade against drinking—often accompanied by anti-prostitution and anti-divorce sentiment—appealed more to the middle class than to other classes. Farmers were generally disinterested, as were urban workers and upper classes. Some felt saloons had a right to be open and that it was not the government's place—nor anyone else's—to regulate what citizens drank. Many workers saw these discussions as remote from their day-to-day problems.

Some of the upper class agreed with eliminating alcohol, prostitution and divorce. Others did not. Then, there was the subset of businessmen who made a sizable profit from financing breweries, distilleries and equipment, as well as by renting rooms to brothels and saloons. Thus there was a multiclass pushback on anti-saloon measures.

Backed by many Protestant churches, prohibitionists forged an unlikely alliance with Protestant ministers. Prohibitionists tried piecemeal legislation, such as advocating for local laws. These included curtailing saloon hours, forcing Sunday closings on account of the Sabbath, raising license fees and mandating one- and two-mile dry zones around schools and military bases.

In response, Republican leaders felt caught in a bind. On the one hand, many of their constituents were evangelical Protestants who actively backed Prohibition. On the other hand, the remainder of their electorate opposed it. Their districts were filled with thirsty men—many of whom voted. Some politicians thought it best to ignore the issue.

Prohibition laws were most popular in the South and rural North. In New York State, there was a mixed reaction.

ANTI-SALOON LEAGUE

Drawing support from Methodists, Baptists and Congregationalists, the Anti-Saloon League was the most prominent advocacy group for Prohibition. Founded in 1893, it is considered the most successful single-issue lobbying group in U.S. history. It gradually overtook the Women's Christian Temperance Union and the Prohibition Party. It was one of the first advocacy groups focused on a sole issue. The league was sly in applying "pressure politics" in legislative politics. Pressure politics refers to leveraging the media to show legislators that the electorate desires a particular bill. It usually implies backing a politician into a corner; if he or she votes against a proposed bill, there would be a steep political price to pay.

The Anti-Saloon League strung together unlikely partners. These included Democrats and Republicans, suffragettes, powerful industry men like Andrew Carnegie and the International Workers of the World. Membership included the NAACP and the Ku Klux Klan. It was a membership of contradictions. This massive partnership commanded the ear of nearly every politician.

Wayne Wheeler, a leader of the Anti-Saloon League, was one of the group's masterminds. To show the mass support for Prohibition, he compiled a list of thirteen thousand businesspeople who supported its passage. The league sent Congress only those telegrams of businesspeople supportive of Prohibition that were signed by different names. This tactic was emblematic of the pressure politics: "We blocked the telegraph wires in Congress for three days. One of our friends sent seventy-five telegrams, each signed differently with the name of one of his subordinates. The campaign was successful. Congress surrendered. The first to bear the white flag was Senator Warren Harding of Ohio. He told us frankly he was opposed to the amendment, but since it was apparent from the telegrams that the business world was demanding it, he would submerge his own opinion and vote for submission."[121]

Financed by annual dues, the league's tactics were so effective that national politicians feared the organization. In fighting for a constitutional amendment, the league employed a sophisticated public relations campaign. Tactics included testifying in hearings, establishing the Scientific Temperance Federation and using patriotism to appeal to constituents on an emotional level. The league also formed the American Issue Publishing House to print leaflets, pamphlets and other advocacy materials. It was said to have "printed so many leaflets—over forty tons of mail per month—that its headquarters in Westerville, Ohio, was the smallest town to have a first-class post office."[122] Contemporary public relations borrows many of these methods.

With the anti-German fervor of World War I, the Anti-Saloon League also connected Germans to breweries and therefore to saloons and bars. It was an association meant to turn public sentiment away from alcohol further.

The Anti-Saloon League believed its advocacy—no matter the tactics—were righteous, as it was "bringing about God's will." Any politician who dared oppose the league was said to regret it. The league's printing press distributed propaganda to every city and town. Wayne Wheeler knew how to focus on one issue and to drive a wedge with it by forcing politicians to choose sides.

The league also knew that if it was asking the government to ban alcohol and give up the excise tax, it would need to find a way to replace that income. The answer lay in another social reform: the income tax. With an alliance already formed, social reformers and Protestant pastors helped bring about the Sixteenth Amendment. The revenue from taxing Americans would more than compensate for the lost excise tax from the ban on the purchase and sale of alcohol, they reasoned.

An alliance of rural evangelicals and the middle class achieved success in the South. In 1907, Georgia and Alabama went dry. Oklahoma, Mississippi and North Carolina soon followed, as did Tennessee. So did various locales in Connecticut and Illinois. A federal constitutional amendment, though, was still more than a decade away.

Cartoon shows Mr. Dry (the cartoonist's puritanical symbol for the Prohibitionists) holding an umbrella labeled "Anti-Saloon League," trying to shield a vast pile of money labeled "Political contributions." In February 1923, William H. Anderson, New York State superintendent of the Anti-Saloon League, refused to answer questions regarding the misuse of funds. Anderson was later convicted, and the adverse publicity caused prominent donors, such as the Rockefellers, to withdraw support. *Cartoon by Rollin Kirby, Library of Congress, Prints and Photographs Division, Alfred Bendiner Memorial Collection.*

Finally, after years of political maneuvering, negotiating and strong-arming, the amendment was passed on January 16, 1919. The Eighteenth Amendment to the U.S. Constitution made it "illegal to manufacture, sell, or transport intoxicating liquors for beverage purposes." In practice, law enforcement prosecuted a small percentage who defied the new law. Police arrested about seven thousand Prohibition breakers in New York City from 1921 to 1923. However, very few of these resulted in convictions.[123]

Prohibition turned out to have numerous unintended consequences. First, the loss of tax revenue to states was marked. With a great proportion of New York City's state revenue from liquor taxes, the city was in a budget shortfall.

It gave rise to a new kind of underground bar. Backroom speakeasies dotted New York City as fronts for serving alcoholic beverages. Also, the number of registered pharmacists tripled during this period. The new law permitted pharmacists to "prescribe" whiskey for many types of ailments.

Perhaps the greatest unintended consequence of Prohibition was that it caused American society to rethink its values. Many questioned the moral code. The Jazz Age and Roaring Twenties were ushered in. Liquor consumption skyrocketed among groups like young women, who had previously drunk little.

Ken Burns's documentary *Prohibition* explains this paradox:

> *The culmination of nearly a century of activism, Prohibition was intended to improve, even to ennoble, the lives of all Americans, to protect individuals, families, and society at large from the devastating effects of alcohol abuse. But the enshrining of a faith-driven moral code in the Constitution paradoxically caused millions of Americans to rethink their definition of morality. Thugs became celebrities, responsible authority was rendered impotent.*
>
> *Social mores in place for a century were obliterated. Prohibition turned law-abiding citizens into criminals, made a mockery of the justice system, caused illicit drinking to seem glamorous and fun, encouraged neighborhood gangs to become national crime syndicates, permitted government officials to bend and sometimes even break the law, and fostered cynicism and hypocrisy that corroded the social contract all across the country.*[124]

PROHIBITION IN NEW YORK STATE

Five years after Congress passed Prohibition, New York City had an estimated one hundred thousand speakeasies. New York was nicknamed the "City on a Still." Corruption was rampant. Speakeasies and nightclubs bought protection by paying off law enforcement officers. Payoffs extended to politicians and even to some judges. With seven thousand arrests resulting in almost no convictions, payoffs were likely part of that reason. Politicians were also hypocrites. With many railing against alcohol, those same people were found in speakeasies during raids.

New York State was a central place for bootlegging. Off the coast of New York City, ships lined up to transfer their illicit cargoes onto speedboats in the middle of the night. Northern New York State was also a popular bootlegging area, as the St. Lawrence River separated New York State from Canada. It was prime geography for illegally transporting booze. Many murders and hijackings occurred here too.

Residents of New York State came to see Prohibition as impossible to enforce and creating more problems than it solved. The New York State Legislature eventually called for a constitutional convention to overturn Prohibition.

BLOW TO PROGRESSIVES

With Prohibition in place, but ineffectively enforced, one observer noted, America had hardly freed itself from the scourge of alcohol abuse—instead, the "drys" had their law, while the "wets" had their liquor.

By the late 1920s, President Herbert Hoover referred to Prohibition as a "great social and economic experiment, noble in motive and far-reaching in purpose." It became known as the "noble experiment." Despite the spin of politicians, some social reformers and church leaders, the experiment had failed.

Its supporters had misread human nature and consumer economics. They had naively expected consumers to shift their spending from alcohol to clothing and household goods. They thought neighborhoods would appreciate greatly in value as they would be "cleaned up" from the closure of noisy saloons. Consumer packaged goods firms like Wrigley's chewing gum and Coca-Cola were expecting sales to take off. They thought thirsty consumers would turn toward their brands in the absence of readily available and legal alcohol. Theaters thought more patrons would attend their shows out of boredom now that their bars were closed. They were all wrong.

In reality, many restaurants could not make a profit in the absence of selling high-markup liquor. Attendance decreased in theaters and other

A parody of the death of drinking alcohol with the passage of Prohibition. Though farcical, the photo shows the fervent opposition many had to the passage of Prohibition. *Library of Congress, Division of Prints and Photographs.*

entertainment venues. With the closing of bars, restaurants, distilleries and breweries, many lost their jobs. Across the supply chain, employees lost jobs, including farmers and harvesters of wheat and barley, brewers, coopers, truck drivers and bartenders. These workers, therefore, had much less disposable income to spend on other goods and services.

Prohibition's effects were felt not only among consumers and producers but also by state and federal governments. With limited income tax, governments were overly reliant on alcohol excise tax. In New York, historians estimate nearly 75 percent of the state revenue was derived from liquor taxes. On a federal level, the government gave up about $11 billion in tax revenue when Prohibition went into effect. At the same time, governments' costs soared to enforce Prohibition.

Beneficiaries of Prohibition were those who could legally dispense alcohol or do so in secret. Pharmacies in New York State tripled as bootleggers realized that they could run a pharmacy as a front for their illegal liquor-dealing business. According to several accounts, enrollments increased at places of worship where obtaining wine for their congregations was legal. Others learned to make liquor at home.

But the real effect was beyond economics. Social Progressives had wanted to curtail excessive drinking and domestic altercations that would result. Yet some actually drank more, obtaining their liquor through the underground market, such as in speakeasies. Many police officers and other law enforcement were paid off. Organized crime soared. The environment launched the careers of gangsters Al Capone and Lucky Luciano, among others. Public trust in government eroded.

Many reformers and ministers had viewed liquor as the source of poverty, domestic strife, industrial accidents, criminality and corruption. On the amendment's passage, supporters declared, "Men will walk upright. The slums will be a thing of the past." But reformers did not understand human nature—that to take away something people want will only inspire them to find new ways of obtaining it. The social ills that reformers had thought would be cured through Prohibition were largely made worse.

CURTAILING PROSTITUTION AND DIVORCES

Besides outlawing the purchase and sale of alcohol, reformers also set their sights on stopping prostitution and curtailing divorce. Their efforts yielded mixed results. The United States agreed to abolish the "White slave trade," the alleged transnational traffic of women. Legislators also slapped steep fines and prison sentences on employers of immigrant prostitutes. Reformers won enactment of criminal statutes targeted at pimps and brothel keepers who profited from the prostitution trade.

Some preachers saw young men frequenting prostitutes as the natural outcome from delayed marriage. The pastors reasoned that by putting off marriage, men needed to find an outlet. Thus, laws to punish brothels would address the symptom but not the cause. Walter Gladden noted, "When young men postponed marriage, one of the inevitable consequences was the increase of social immorality. I do not believe that there is any remedy for this social disease but the restoration of a more wholesome sentiment concerning this whole subject of family life. The morality of what we call our respectable classes needs toning up all along this line."[125]

Reformers were less successful in decreasing divorce rates. The organization of this movement was weaker. Its leader, Sam Dike, was a Congregational minister from Vermont. He helped establish the National

Divorce Reform League in the 1880s. The organization, though, failed to attract much attention.

Some states had lax divorce laws. So, those from states with stricter laws simply migrated to those states with more relaxed laws. New York State employed stricter divorce laws with narrow definitions of what was legal grounds for separation. So, some divorcing New Yorkers left for states with more lenient divorce laws. Ultimately, there was not much public interest in this issue. Social scientists also advanced the argument that tighter laws would not lessen the divorce rate. Moreover, the middle class did not feel threatened by divorce laws the way it did by the saloon or the brothel. Even strict puritans understood that sometimes divorce was a necessary evil. One reformer noted, "I do not favor divorce, but it is better to separate than bring up children of drunkards or licentious fathers."

In the early decades of the twentieth century, the divorce rate surprisingly climbed, disappointing social reformers. Consequently, reformers began to shift away from moral judgments about family life, drinking and marriage. Many of their efforts in this domain did not prove effective. Plus, much of the public wondered why they needed to be lectured to about how to live their lives. So, reformers turned their efforts toward economic and political struggles like improving housing, labor and suffrage for women.

The passage of Prohibition was a key accomplishment during the Progressive Era (1890–1920). However, its unintended consequences, and ultimately its repeal in 1933, cast a shadow on Progressives for overreaching into citizens' lives. Some of their other accomplishments would be received more positively and would change society for the better. These developments included an infrastructure that would transform big cities and the conservation of land and parks.

Part VII

INFRASTRUCTURE, LAND MANAGEMENT AND ANIMAL RIGHTS

Transformation of New York State

Between 1898 and 1913, the landscape of the city would transform beyond recognition. Both residents and newcomers needed to adapt to profound changes. New York City would grow in ways no one could have imagined. The once tranquil city's population jumped from 814,000 in 1860 to 5.6 million in 1920. Part of this was the Great Migration of Black people from the South. Many sought to escape the oppressive Jim Crow South and find better jobs up North. New York City's Black population grew exponentially from 1890 to 1920.

New York City itself also grew through annexation. In 1897, it annexed forty towns, cities and neighborhoods in Manhattan, Brooklyn, Queens, Staten Island and the Bronx. This gave the bustling city its five boroughs. The plan was almost twenty-five years in the making. In 1873, citizens discussed a "Greater New York City" by joining Brooklyn and New York.

In the end, it was Brooklyn's elite who resisted the merger more than those from other boroughs. They were afraid of paying higher taxes for what they saw as Manhattan's issues. They also feared government corruption from the still powerful Tammany Hall. Despite these misgivings, the measure for the Greater New York City was passed in 1897.

The subway opening in 1904 allowed residents to spread throughout the boroughs and commute to work. Small service businesses increasingly opened in outer boroughs to service these incoming residents.

Another major factor that influenced the population was the largest influx of immigrants the United States had ever seen. To accommodate these large numbers, a new processing center was needed. For decades, immigrants to the

Immigrants arrive at Castle Garden, the key processing center before the opening of Ellis Island. One reason for the change was corruption at Castle Clinton. *Collection of Maggie Land Blanck.*

1892

Infrastructure, Land Management and Animal Rights

United States had come through Castle Gardens at the foot of Manhattan. By 1890, the one-time concert hall was overwhelmed by the wave of new immigrants. Work had begun on a massive new structure on an abandoned ammunition dump. It would become known as Ellis Island. In December 1900, the massive complex was finally complete. Built to accommodate five hundred thousand per year, it would process up to twelve thousand per day or triple its capacity. In thirty years, twelve million would stream through its winding rooms hoping to find political and economic sanctuary in the rapidly expanding United States. More than four million would permanently settle in New York City, tripling its population.

By law, immigration officials had to turn back polygamists, criminals, paupers and anyone with a disability, heart condition or contagious disease. Future New York City mayor Fiorello La Guardia, who was working as an interpreter on Ellis Island, witnessed devastated families turned back by immigrant officials. The scenes left an indelible impression on him. This harrowing experience of being turned away happened to relatively few immigrants, though. In the end, fewer than 2 percent were turned back.

One in four arrivals took a ferry to an island that they would never leave again. They saw Manhattan's skyline, which made some feel they were in heaven. They asked rhetorically, "Is this a city on earth or in heaven?"

INFRASTRUCTURE CHANGES

As the city swelled in population, its infrastructure was about to be transformed in a way it could not imagine. Thomas Edison was granted a patent for his incandescent light bulb on January 27, 1880. With his lighting innovations, Edison soon signed a contract with New York City to provide outdoor lighting in lower Manhattan. He built an electric power plant on Pearl Street in lower Manhattan. In 1882, he flipped a switch to illuminate one square mile around Wall Street.

Over the next few years, outdoor lighting became the standard in New York. Gaslights were on their way out. The question was how to adopt this for the indoors. Owners of posh restaurants, hotels and office buildings introduced it. Suddenly, people could do more night activities.

Electricity offered a cleaner solution too. As the number of horses on the streets dropped, New York streets became cleaner, as there were fewer horse droppings. New York was transformed by electricity. Housewives were freed from laborious clothes washing by use of the washing machine.

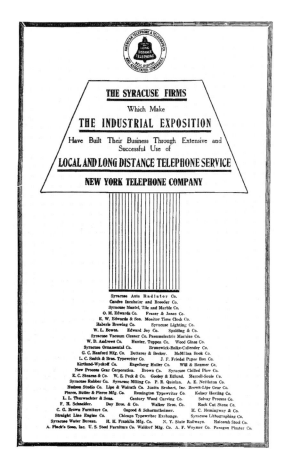

Advertisement for industrial exposition in Syracuse, New York, for long distance and local telephone service in 1913. The ad shows the industrial and infrastructure expansion in upstate New York cities like Syracuse. *Courtesy of Syracuse Journal.*

Steel also transformed the city. Skyscrapers soared into the sky. Corporations loved showcasing their logos and brands on these imposing structures. In 1903, on Fifth Avenue and Twenty-Third Street, the twenty-one-story Flatiron Building was erected. Five years later, the Singer Building was erected and was double the height of the Flatiron. That was surpassed by the fifty-story Metropolitan Life Building two years later on Madison Square. About 550 buildings in lower Manhattan were ten stories or higher. New Yorkers loved these buildings. Mankind's new frontier was in the sky. Some called it the "poetry of the modern world."

Upstate and western New York cities were transforming, as well. Telephone companies and newly formed utility companies took out advertisements in periodicals to showcase their expansion. One example was a long-running ad from the New York Telephone Company showing how their service benefited Syracuse-area firms in central New York State.

AUTOMOBILES OFFER NEW FREEDOMS

Workplaces also transformed from the advent of electricity. Factory owners now able to operate at night made some of their employees work during the new "graveyard shift." Owners could maximize their capital output, but workers were displeased. They had to work at off-hours and disrupt their lives. In 1913, Henry Ford introduced the assembly line. This industrial innovation was made possible because of electricity.

Cars were seen as toys for the rich. Most Americans did not like them. Many New Yorkers saw them as a menace to horses and pedestrians. In 1909, though, Henry Ford and his small team perfected the Model T in their makeshift Piquette Plant in Detroit, Michigan. Making each car was extremely laborious and, therefore, very expensive. Ford's goal was to optimize the production process to drive out cost. Assembly lines had previously existed. Ford, though, pioneered the continuously moving line where workers repeating the same task for each unit had a specified amount of time to complete that task to keep the line going. Signs in the nascent Piquette Plant read, "Keep the line moving!" By decreasing production times and subsequent costs, the average working person could afford to purchase the car. By 1914, a large workforce in Highland Park, Michigan, was turning out an unprecedented number of Model Ts per day. Ford had offered a rare five dollars per day, thereby driving up wages at other factories. On the downside, the work was tedious, with some employees longing for the bygone days of craftmanship where one worked on a product from start to finish.

Suddenly, cars were for mass consumption. Assembly line workers took just two hours and forty minutes per car, decreasing production times dramatically from twelve hours. By 1920, Ford and his mechanical engineers reduced production time further to about ninety minutes. These production efficiencies brought down prices to about $345. Competitors copied these production tools.

Factory owners in New York took notice of this moving assembly line. New industries were created or expanded. The arrival of automobiles revived steal and rubber productions. Light manufacturing of clothing and food took off in Manhattan.

The car's effect on social class and urbanization was marked. The car brought freedom to many New Yorkers. Despite the car's limitations, some car owners and passengers saw this new vehicle as a way to free themselves of timetables and fixed routes. *Harper's Weekly* noted that the motor vehicle embodied "the feeling of independence—the freedom from timetables, from fixed and inflexible routes, from the proximity of other human beings…the ability to go where and when one wills…and the satisfaction that comes from a knowledge that one need ask favors or accommodation from no one nor trespass on anybody's property or privacy."

For Progressives, the automobile had the potential to liberate the middle class, and possibly the poor, from cities. Some envisioned that the vehicle would break down class distinctions. But their vision was shortsighted. In reality, the high expense of the automobile was affordable only to the affluent. Moreover, early automobile owners were preoccupied with speed, which many Progressives came to see as dangerous. Woodrow Wilson, for example, exclaimed in 1906, "Of all the menaces of today, the worst is the reckless driving of automobiles." Also, the early automobile caused more friction between urban and rural dwellers. Many rural residents in places like upstate New York resented urban drivers coming into their towns and near their farms.

As the second decade of the twentieth century wore on, the Model T prototype and other early vehicles dropped steeply in price. Consequently, cars became more affordable. Farmers also started to adopt them and saw them as a way out of the isolation of rural life. For female drivers, the promise was to break down the gender segregation of modern life. Women interacted more with the world outside their home and immediate neighborhood.

Not everyone thought this "liberation" for women was positive. Steeped in Victorian values, the budding middle class had mixed feelings about women taking on more independence. On the one hand, they encouraged progress. But there was a sense among some men and women that the woman's role in the home should be undisturbed. Indeed, some women lambasted female drivers as "mannish." One man said, "The automobile has given women too much confidence and has had a sad effect on motherhood." These attitudes affected usage. By 1914, women were only about 15 percent of registered car owners in major cities. Driving was somewhat dangerous, as few roads were paved. In medium and large cities, cars had to share the roads with horses and trollies.

These attitudes contrasted with automobile manufacturer marketing motivations. To enhance its customer base, Ford tried to acquire female customers. Ford's advertising declared the "happy change" of women driving. One ad read, "The automobile has broadened her horizon—increased her pleasures—given new vigor to her body—made neighbors of faraway friends—and multiplied tremendously her range of activity. It is a real weapon in the changing order."[126]

As consumers started to drive more cars, that meant they took up more space on roads. In cities, cars displaced play areas for street kids. In Manhattan, autos killed over one thousand children by World War I. Working-class neighborhoods discouraged cars from driving in their neighborhoods by throwing stones and firecrackers. Over time, though, cars won the battle. This meant kids lacked a place to safely play. The reformers' answer was to build playgrounds. Lillian Wald of the Henry Street Settlement pioneered the concept to take kids off crowded, dangerous streets. The Henry Street Settlement, still in its present location, offered a playground.

SUBWAYS AND TRAIN STATIONS LINK THE CITY

In 1901, few modes connected the island of Manhattan to its surrounding areas. There was the majestic and gracious Brooklyn Bridge connecting Manhattan and Brooklyn. That was the only East River crossing. The next one, the Williamsburg Bridge, opened in 1903. There was only one train line, called the New York Central Railroad, owned by robber baron and one of the world's richest men, William Vanderbilt, descendant of the famed Cornelius Vanderbilt. This railroad had the deep competitive advantage of coming into Manhattan, while others could not. Its trains came from upstate New York and ran through the east bank of the Hudson, near the Harlem River, and into Manhattan. The New York Central had bridges over the Harlem River at the head of Park Avenue and at Spuyten Duyvil in the Bronx, their current locations. There were several road bridges over the Harlem River, including the oldest at Kingsbridge. There was also the aqueduct at the High Bridge, built in 1848, which served as a link in the Croton Aqueduct bringing fresh water into Manhattan from the Bronx.

A frenzy of construction went on above ground, linking the boroughs. The Interborough Rapid Transit System transformed the city's transportation system. It would become the greatest subway system in the world. It was built in just four years. In 1904, it was the most extensive system in the nation. It was to provide robust transportation and access for the suburban populations in outlying boroughs.

The only functional railroad line during this period was William Vanderbilt's New York Central. William was not known for his concern for passengers. History has shown him as ruthless and greedy. He is said to have remarked, "Let the public be damned." He succeeded in connecting his railway to Manhattan, a feat the Pennsylvania Railroad had long been trying.

For decades, one of the most powerful companies in the nation struggled to reach Manhattan's elusive shores. Executives tried many tactics, such as building a bridge over the Hudson River, but none came to fruition. Finally, in the late 1890s, Pennsylvania Railroad leaders Alexander Cassatt and Samuel Rea dared to pioneer two feats. First, they would lay down tracks in the turbulent Hudson and East Rivers to reach Manhattan, which had become a global hub of commerce. They were visionaries, as tunneling was a concept few had heard of. Second, they would build a monumental station in the heart of one of New York's most notorious, corrupt and vice-filled neighborhoods. It would be a station that would do more than transport passengers. It would ennoble the public. For the passerby, whether rich or poor, it was as if ancient Rome had been brought to their backyard. It was a station that would inspire the world, even if only for half a century.

In 1910, based on the Gare d'Orsay train station in Paris and the Baths of Caracalla in Rome, the original Pennsylvania Station was built.

In 1908, in New York City's Tenderloin District at Thirty-Second between Seventh and Eighth Avenues, a gaping hole was made for the construction of the Pennsylvania Station. Modeled after the Baths of Caracalla, it was said that for New Yorkers it was like having ancient Rome in their backyard. *Wikimedia Commons.*

A side entrance of Pennsylvania Station, built in 1910. It was the crowning achievement that finally connected Manhattan to the rest of the United States through the tunnels under the Hudson River. *Library of Congress, Division of Prints and Photographs.*

Through engineering feats unrivaled by any, the island of Manhattan was finally connected to the North American continent for the first time since the Ice Age.

The rooms were in a classical style harking back to ancient Rome. The station was considered the most handsome in the world. Novelist Thomas Wolfe, known for *You Can't Go Home Again*, remarked on its beauty:

> *The station was murmurous with the immense space and distant sound of time. Great slanted beams of moated light fell ponderously throughout the station's floor and the calm voice of time hovered along the ceilings and walls of that mighty room. Distilled out of the voices and movements of the people who swarmed beneath. Here, as nowhere else on earth, men were brought together for a moment for the beginning or end of their innumerable journeys. Here, one saw their greetings and farewells. Here, in a single instant, one got the entire picture of human destiny. Men came and went. They passed and vanished. All were moving through the moments of their lives. But the voice of time remained aloof and unperturbed: a drowsy and eternal murmur below the immense and distance roof.*

Three years after Pennsylvania Station opened in Manhattan's West Side, the Vanderbilts opened a contemporary version of Grand Central, which stands to the present day. Known as less customer centric than the Pennsylvania Railroad, William Vanderbilt's Central Railway was Pennsylvania Railroad's primary competition. The first incarnation of Grand Central Station opened in 1871 by Cornelius Vanderbilt. Built at Forty-Second Street, it was a somewhat remote area at the time. But Vanderbilt likely chose it due to the pressure of keeping his steam locomotives away from population centers. Or he might have seen the area as ripe for development. His depot was to service all three lines that Vanderbilt acquired: New York Central, Hudson River and Harlem River. (Those three lines remain more or less at present-day Grand Central Station.)

Grand Central was a hub for several railroad lines entering Manhattan. It was known for its *L* shape. Yet the capacity was limited. As the number of railroads grew, it became clear that a larger building was needed. Around the turn of the century, the building was replaced with a more expansive one with six stories. Its name was Grand Central Station because it merged three individual stations into a single terminal. "The red brick walls, with their cast-iron embellishments, were stripped and resurfaced with handsome granite, and the three mansard roofs were removed."[127] The main waiting room was bright from a steel-ribbed skylight. This rendition of Grand Central would last from 1899 to 1913, when it was replaced by the current structure, which was considered more user-friendly and safer.

The expansion of railroads ignited the New York economy. Suddenly, goods could be transported quickly and easily. Railroads markedly reduced transportation costs. Historian Martin Albro proclaimed, "In all of the human past, no event has so swiftly and profoundly changed the basic order of things as had the coming of the railroad."[128] However, as Albro points out, the changes were also catastrophic, as the carnage it produced in people and property from accidents and collateral damage was unprecedented.[129]

INFRASTRUCTURE AND CORPORATE EXPANSION IN UPSTATE AND WESTERN NEW YORK

During the Progressive Era, upstate and western New York cities expanded markedly from technological innovation. By the early twentieth century in Rochester, New York, three companies based on optical and film innovations proliferated. First, Bausch and Lomb had started in 1853. After forty years, the company had a breakthrough in the early 1890s, with the introduction of optical lenses used for eyeglasses, microscopes and binoculars. Teddy Roosevelt's expansion of the U.S. Army and Naval fleet helped the company grow precipitously. The company produced a high-precision lens for optical measurement. Secondly, in the 1880s and into the 1890s, George Eastman's Kodak had revolutionized photography, making the process easier, cleaner and more reliable. Kodak's innovations changed the way Americans saw their news—suddenly, photos became a key part of news delivery. Thirdly, Xerox was founded in 1906 in Rochester, New York, as the Haloid Photographic Company. It manufactured and distributed photographic paper before becoming Xerox decades later.

Corning, a maker of specialty glass and ceramics, moved its headquarters and research facilities to southwestern New York State in 1908. This company transformed the sleepy western New York town.

Transportation evolved in these cities, as well. As one example, in 1900, the Albany Union Station opened and served about ninety-six trains per day. Stations like these across upstate cities allowed for easier passenger and

Albany Union Station was built in 1900 as part of the infrastructure expansion in upstate New York. *Library of Congress, Prints and Photographs Division.*

Above: The Riveted Arch Bridge built over the Genesee River in Rochester, New York, in 1890 as part of the infrastructure development of upstate and western New York. *Historic American Building Survey, Library of Congress, Division of Prints and Photographs.*

Left: Famed architects Lewis Sullivan and Dankmar Adler designed the Prudential Building in downtown Buffalo, completed in 1895. The early skyscraper manifested Sullivan's belief that "Form must follow function." *Wikimedia Commons.*

Downtown Buffalo in 1900. Like other cities in the state, Buffalo's infrastructure and cultural offerings increased markedly during the Progressive Era. *Library of Congress, Prints and Photographs Division.*

freight rail transportation from Albany to Buffalo. Bridges over rivers were built across New York State to allow for easier passage. One famous example was the Arch Bridge over the Genessee River in Rochester.

Downtown Buffalo also expanded during this period, with skyscrapers and important architectural buildings. One was the Prudential Building, erected by noted architects Lewis Sullivan and Dankmar Adler in 1895. The building would serve as a prototype of other office buildings and towers in terms of how space is divided to optimize work processes.

As the nation's infrastructure was rapidly expanding, there was also a movement Teddy Roosevelt spearheaded to conserve land and parks, as well as antiquities. It would become the forerunner to the modern environmental public policy program.

Conservation of Parks and Antiquities and Animal Protections

A nother hallmark of the Progressive Era was conservation efforts. Realizing the great public value in natural lands, reformers fought to preserve parks, forests and wildlife. They aimed to curtail one of the effects of the Industrial Revolution: overconsuming natural resources. John Muir's Sierra Club, founded in California, was the first major conservationist organization in the United States. He advocated for forest protection. Conservationists also advanced an economic argument. If land was over-grazed, rivers over-fished, or forests over-cut, their value to future generations was at stake.

Though much of the conservation efforts focused on western states, New York State was an important part of this movement because that is where the main champion, Theodore Roosevelt, was from. The onetime rancher was a naturalist, bird lover and nature preserver. He wrote, "When I hear of the destruction of a species, I feel just as if all the works of some great writer had perished." He implored individuals to subject his whim for the preservation of nature. "In the past, we have admitted the right of the individual to injure the Republic for his present profit," he noted in 1901. "The time has come for a change."

Theodore Roosevelt was an improbable outdoorsman. A frail, sickly boy, he exhibited a strong interest in taxidermy. He started a collection of stuffed specimens and later donated some to the American Museum of Natural History in New York City. Several years later, the "skinny, young, spectacled dude from New York" traveled to the Dakota Territory to hunt bison in

New York State Conservation Committee Book in 1913. Thanks to Teddy Roosevelt and other preservationists, New York State put more attention to environmental concerns during the Progressive Era. *Flickr Commons.*

1883. His adventure was arduous, and the landscape was unforgiving. Still, the majesty of the prairies and mysteries of the outdoors inspired the young and still unknown man. He took on a great appreciation for nature in all its species. He loved the land and purchased a ranch in the Badlands, where he returned to ride and hunt. He vowed to preserve the land. He later wrote a book describing his times in the West.

These personal experiences inspired the future New York politician to preserve camping grounds, game reserves and new forests. Once president, he ordered the Agricultural Forest Bureau to take on accountability for land preservation and passed executive declarations to protect public lands.

President Teddy Roosevelt would emerge as one of the most influential advocates for conservation in U.S. history. While president, he ushered in a tide of conservation legislation. He "used his authority to establish 150 national forests, 51 federal bird reserves, four national game preserves, five national parks, and 18 national monuments on over 230 million acres of public land."[130] New York State's Adirondack Mountains were one of the first testing grounds for conservation in the East. Camping in the Adirondacks became increasingly popular.

For Roosevelt, protection of lands was personal. As president, he left a national speaking tour to spend two weeks camping in Yellowstone National

Above: An open camp in the Adirondacks in northern New York State around 1910. Outdoor camping became more popular from the promotion of Teddy Roosevelt encouraging environmental preservation and enjoyment. *Wikimedia Commons.*

Left: Teddy Roosevelt at Yosemite National Park. His love for the land inspired the beginning of the environmental movement. *Library of Congress, Prints and Photographs Division.*

Park, visited the Grand Canyon to advocate its protection and slept out under the stars in Yosemite with John Muir, a keen environmentalist who became known as the "Father of the National Parks."

But the conservation movement met with predictable resistance. Anti-conservationists opposed any restriction of land, forest or park use. They saw nothing wrong with unrestricted development.

PROTECTION OF ENVIRONMENT

In the late nineteenth century, bird feathers seemed indispensable to women's hat fashions. Some hats even included entire stuffed birds: "The long, white plumes of egrets had become more valuable than gold. To satisfy the demands of this latest fashion trend, more than 5 million birds a year were being slaughtered; nearly 95 percent of Florida's shorebirds had been killed by plume hunters."[131]

In the early years of the twentieth century, in response, environmental organizations like the Audubon Society sprang up. The nascent Audubon's mission was to protect the waterbird populations. At first, it held a series of teas for wealthy Boston fashion-conscious women, dissuading them from buying hats with bird feathers. However, the campaign was unsuccessful, as most did not change their hat-buying habits.

The group then turned its efforts to fighting the millinery trade, which used bird feathers to make high-end hats. By 1898, Audubon societies emerged on the state level, including New York. The Audubon Society sought to encourage the public to think of animals, birds and land as precious and limited resources. It also discouraged rampant hunting in favor of environmentally educational activities. For instance, the society dissuaded participants of the traditional Christmas Side Hunt, in which hunters competed on who could kill as many mammals and birds. Instead, the society created an all-volunteer holiday census of early winter bird populations.

These early successes brought the founding of the National Audubon Society, which emphasized the protection of birds like herons, gulls and water birds. More than saving a species, the society and conservationists set out to change public opinion. Before the Progressive Era, there had been little environmental awareness. Most of the public had never been exposed to it. Conservationists needed to show the importance of their movement. In this, "an unlikely champion stepped forward in the form of Congressman John F. Lacey. Despite being part of a group of die-hard conservatives, when it came to defending wildlife, Lacey was one of the most Progressive politicians of his day. After years of ceaseless effort, he won passage of the Lacey Bird and Game Act of 1900. The bill made it a federal crime to transport birds killed in violation of any state law, and soon government agents were confiscating huge shipments of bird skins and feathers."[132]

But the act had limited effect, as many poachers ignored it. Shockingly, in some cases, poachers even killed wardens who were sent to enforce the law in wildlife refuges.

The Audubon's advocacy efforts paid off in 1910 in New York State with landmark legislation. In 1910, the New York State Legislature passed the Audubon Plumage Law, which outlawed the sale or possession of feathers from protected bird species.

This conservation movement received another strong boost in 1918 from President Woodrow Wilson's signing of the Migratory Bird Treaty Act (MBTA), which protected wild North American birds. The bill's passage ushered in bird sanctuaries in seven states, including New York, where scientists could study bird populations to improve their conservation efforts.

ANIMAL PROTECTION

The late nineteenth century also saw the opening of agencies devoted to the protection of animals. New York was at the center. In 1866, philanthropist and diplomat Henry Bergh founded the American Society for the Prevention of Cruelty to Animals (ASPCA). Bergh became sympathetic to the plight of animals while serving in a diplomatic post at the Russian court of Czar Alexander II. He noticed farmers and peasants beating their workhorses cruelly. He was inspired by the Royal Society for the Prevention of Cruelty to Animals and thought he could replicate it in New York. Bergh gave impassioned speeches where he noted that animal rights transcend party and political lines. He implored representatives to sign his Declaration of the Rights of Animals.

His advocacy paid off. The New York State Legislature passed the charter incorporating the ASPCA. Shortly after that, the nation's first anti-cruelty law was passed. Bergh also visited slaughterhouses and other animal venues to ensure that animals were treated properly. In 1888, virtually all states passed anti-cruelty laws. The ASPCA also served as a model for the newly formed New York Society for the Prevention of Cruelty to Children.

Another New York–based animal rights organization that reformers started was the Humane Society. It was started in 1904 to protect horses against abuse. The organization battled for laws to punish abusive owners and lobbied for watering holes for horses in streets and parks. One ad read, "Don't forget that your horse also suffers from the heat and should be watered often. The Humane Society of New York establishes stations throughout New York City and Brooklyn, where drivers may secure water without charge of any kind. Light summer bridles are also placed free of charge on horses."[133]

The society later opened a free medical clinic and small adoption center for cats and dogs, which is still operational today. Beyond delivering services, these early New York–based animal societies reshaped the public perception of animals. They challenged New Yorkers to view animals as requiring and deserving fair treatment and ensuring that their basic needs were met—just like with humans.

Preserving Ancient Ruins

Conservation efforts extended beyond preserving natural resources to protecting archaeological sites and antiquity findings. This movement gained steam when in 1889 rancher brothers accidentally came across ancient ruins in the cliffs of Mesa Verde in Colorado. Stumbling into history, the brothers sold thousands of artifacts to museums. They sought to protect the ruins they found by requesting the government to make Mesa Verde a federal park. The government declined.

Not long after, sensing an opportunity, a Swedish archaeologist sent a huge shipment of the Mesa Verde artifacts overseas. Since there was no law in place to preserve antiquities, this act was legal. Unschooled formally in archaeology, the brothers continued their quest to find other archaeological ruins. Academic archaeologists tried to stop them. The brothers offered to give up any claim to ruins they found if the federal government agreed to protect the ruins.

Though more interested in protecting natural settings than ancient manmade ones, President Roosevelt came to see the value in protecting antiquities and archaeological finds. In response to the recent archaeological findings, on June 29, 1906, he signed a law establishing Mesa Verde National Park. "It was the first park created specifically to celebrate a prehistoric culture and its people and marked a broadening of the park idea. But while Mesa Verde had been saved, there was no law protecting any of the other ancient ruins scattered throughout the Southwest."[134] Soon after, the Act of Preservation of American Antiquities was passed. The law prohibited any interference with a prehistoric ruin. The Antiquities Act also allowed the president to preserve places that would be called national monuments. Roosevelt used the act to preserve the Grand Canyon, among several other national monuments.

In the final analysis, the conservation movement during the Progressive Era was as much about preserving the environment and antiquities as it was about changing public opinion. Caught up in their day-to-day lives, most U.S. citizens rarely, if ever, thought about these issues. Few buyers of hats with feathers in them considered their effect on water birds. Nor did the public think of how to save the archaeological ruins of an ancient civilization. As a result, these efforts relied on swaying the public's hearts and minds—and those of their elected officials. When Progressive politicians like Teddy Roosevelt championed these causes and organizations like the Audubon Society, the changes slowly took place.

Part VIII

DECLINE OF PROGRESSIVISM

I7

IMPACT OF GREAT WAR

W hen World War I broke out, no one expected the United States to
enter it. The most popular song in 1915 was "I Didn't Raise My Boy
to Be a Soldier." Two years later, George Cohan's "Over There"
became the most popular. That musical popularity transition embodied the
change in American sentiment about the war. Historically, the United States
had tried to stay out of European conflicts.

Pacifists like Jane Addams of Chicago's Hull House and industrialists
like Henry Ford opposed U.S. entry into the war, as did Irish Americans
because entry would mean the United States would be helping the British.
At this time, many Irish Americans had anti-British feelings. Many German
Americans opposed it as well. They did not want to attack their homeland.

In contrast, Teddy Roosevelt supported the entry into the Great War.
Seeing the lack of preparedness, as a private citizen, he helped launch a
training ground in Plattsburgh, New York, in 1915 and 1916, where twenty
thousand troops were prepared. He believed the United States should enter
the war. He saw Woodrow Wilson as a "weak, effeminate man who lectured
on morals rather than acting on them."

Once Wilson decided the United States should enter the war, society
shifted in ways no one expected. When the country started to ship soldiers
abroad, there were concerns over whether businesses could produce enough
goods and services to meet the war's staggering demands. Chief among
these was the ability to transfer weapons, soldiers and equipment via rail.
So, the Wilson administration nationalized parts of the economy. Wilson
created the Railroad Administration to ensure the rail system could meet

Crowds gather in August 1914 in Union Square to protest the Great War. Within a few years, to their dismay, the United States would enter the war. *Library of Congress, Division of Prints and Photographs.*

needs. Pennsylvania Station in New York City, for example, was nationalized during the war, as were many of Pennsylvania Railroad's lines. Wilson also implemented a shipping board to manage a large shipbuilding agenda and a war industries council to look after manufacturing quotas and supplies.

The National Labor Board all but forced private businesses with government contracts to accept the forty-hour workweek, along with safety standards. Ironically, many of the measures were fought for by unions for years. Once the United States entered the Great War, it was the war boards that enforced these measures. Businesses generally did not oppose them. Americans, therefore, enjoyed higher wages and safer workplaces.

On the other hand, Wilson curtailed civil liberties. His Committee on Public Information created propaganda techniques to support the war, leveraging advertising techniques. In June 1917, Wilson signed the Espionage Act, which essentially limited free speech. Writing or speaking out against the war was criminalized. Progressives like Lillian Wald and Jane Addams, pioneers of the Settlement House movement in New York and Chicago, were caught. They opposed the war and marched in demonstrations. Wald's Henry Street Settlement lost much financial support as a result. She was

Massive figure of George Washington displaying his beliefs about patriotism and war. Below him, a small figure leads a peace march of "100 Pacifist Delegates to Washington," saying, "My friends, that militarist jingo is 'way out of date." The cartoon condemns the pacifists who mounted a new campaign to keep the United States out of World War I in February 1917. *Artist Lute Pease, Library of Congress, Prints and Photographs Division.*

THE DEWEY PARADE AS THE VAINGLORIOUS TEDDY SAW IT.

An 1899 cartoon depicting the "vainglorious Teddy" Roosevelt. It mocks what some saw as Teddy's sanctimoniousness. It depicts Theodore Roosevelt with sash labeled "Admiral Teddy" in crowd of Teddy Roosevelt lookalikes. New York City. *Library of Congress, Division of Prints and Photographs.*

caught in a bind between preserving her organization and opposing the war effort. Wald was blacklisted for her dissent.

Finally, on November 11, 1918, an armistice was signed. The losses in the war were tragic but represented a fraction of those suffered by allied countries like Great Britain and France.

THE AFTERMATH OF THE GREAT WAR

During the Great War, unemployment plummeted. Strikes decreased. Unions were recognized. While Americans differed on their view of the United States entering the war, there seemed to be a united front with employers and employees. Finally, workers were getting what they believed was their due.

But when the war ended, employers were not interested in keeping these benefits. Workers responded by striking. In 1919, there was "the greatest wave of strikes in American history to that point. Some 4 million workers walked off their jobs in 3,600 strikes."[135] After a peaceful few years, labor was fraught with unrest and violence.

Red scares were prevalent. New York State's legislature expelled five members for their affiliation with the Socialist Party. But no red revolution emerged. The Russian Revolution made Americans' fear more concrete. They were alarmed by the industrial unrest in 1919. Plus, racial riots broke out in 1919. Without evidence, some of the media and select politicians blamed communists. "Reds Try to Stir Negroes to Revolt," declared the *New York Times*.

J. Edgar Hoover compiled a list of Reds. The government arrested those affiliated with Socialist or Communist Parties. Non-citizens were deported for sedition. On December 21, 1919, they sailed from New York's shores on a ship nicknamed the Soviet Arc: "Just as the sailing of the arc Noah built was a saving for the human race, so the sailing of the Soviet arc was a saving of America."

In the spring of 1919, anarchists sent thirty package bombs to elite political and business leaders. While few detonated, they were proof for some that radicals were trying to tear apart the country. That meant strict measures were needed.

The Red scare also influenced the restriction of immigration. As many blamed immigrants for the failings in the United States, and many Americans were concerned about the flood of new arrivals from the previous four decades, they turned toward a quota-based system.

The Klan also reemerged in 1915 and prospered in the 1920s. D.W. Griffith's film *The Birth of a Nation* brought rise to it. While before the Klan was prominent in the South and mostly anti-Black, in this new form, it was more national and also anti-Jewish, anti-Catholic and anti-immigrant. In New York, there were rallies with no hoods, due to the state law.

Poster for the infamous and first feature-length film, *The Birth of a Nation*. The film was highly controversial for stirring up racist sentiments and reinvigorating the Ku Klux Klan. Based on the book *The Clansman*. *Courtesy of Wikimedia Commons.*

END OF AN ERA

B y the fall of 1920, Warren Harding and Calvin Coolidge were elected. This event, along with others, marked the end of the Progressive Era. Coolidge, who entered the White House after Harding's untimely death, slanted very pro-business. He famously quipped, "The business of America is business." He slowed government regulations, lowered corporate income taxes and gave few rights or acknowledgements to unions.

The 1924 National Origins Act greatly limited immigration. Coolidge noted, "America must be kept American." The Red Scare also led to a return to nationalism. Many started to see the United States' role in World War I as a mistake. This notion led to an isolationist philosophy.

Reformers in New York State, as well as across the county, had accomplished much by 1920. Women achieved the right to vote. Unions had won important concessions from employers. Dangerous workplaces were made safer. Shorter work hours were more commonplace. Government corruption eased with institutions such as Tammany Hall weakened. Monopolies were broken up. Citizens could vote directly for their senators. The introduction of the personal income and estate tax somewhat narrowed wealth disparities. Laws were passed to protect forests, parks and antiquities.

What's more, reformers had shifted the public's view on important matters. They convinced many why a laissez-faire government was no longer the best solution. They showed why regulators needed to reign in businesses. They challenged the prevailing theory of poverty—that it was not necessarily the result of laziness but often due to very challenging situations.

In other ways, some Progressives overplayed their hand. They tried to dictate morality, weighing in on matters like divorce and drinking. Some of the immigrants and working class wondered what gave them the right to tell them how to live their lives. The passage of Prohibition was successful, yet ultimately proved a major failure. White Progressives also failed to address steep racial injustices, turning a blind eye to many of Black Americans' struggles.

After the Great War ended, so did some of the Progressive Era ideals. Businesses opted to return to the prewar labor conditions and long hours imposed on workers. Congress curtailed unrestricted immigration. Settlement houses, once a great novelty, lost some of their support in the ensuing decades. The government was suspicious of outside political movements.

The public was moving on. What was once a reaction to the Gilded Age seemed out of step in the go-go 1920s. New Yorkers were dancing to jazz, speculating in the stock market, building skyscrapers and making a quick buck. Presidents Calvin Coolidge and Warren Harding encouraged a hands-off approach to business regulation. The Progressive Era seemed from another age—one that was no longer relevant.

The Progressive Era was closing in 1920. But the pendulum of history is always swinging. What no one knew then was that in under a decade, the intoxicating 1920s would come to an abrupt halt and lead to the greatest depression in U.S. history. That would usher in a new series of reforms—the New Deal—that would revisit the ideals of the Progressive Era for a new generation.

NOTES

Chapter 1

1. O'Donnell, "America in the Gilded Age."
2. Andrew Carnegie, *The Gospel of Wealth and Other Timely Essays*, ed. Edward Kirkland (Cambridge, MA: Harvard University Press, 1962).
3. Frederick Townsend Martin, *Things I Remember* (New York: John Lane Company, 1913), 280–81; *New York Times*, January 23 and February 2, 1897; "Dr. Rainsord's Warning to the Rich," *Literary Digest* 14 (February 6, 1897): 417–18.
4. Jackson Lears, "Guilded Age."
5. Paul Kaplan, *Lillian Wald: America's Great Social and Healthcare Reformer* (Gretna, LA: Pelican Publishing, 2018).
6. Judith Smith, *Family Connections* (Albany, NY: SUNY Press, 1985), 23–35.
7. Kathy Peiss, *Cheap Amusements: Working Women and Leisure in Turn-of-the-Century New York* (Philadelphia: N.p., 1986).
8. E.C. Moore, "The Social Value of the Saloon," *American Journal of Sociology* 3 (July 1897): 1–12
9. John Tebbel, *The Inheritors: A Study of America's Great Fortunes and What Happened to Them* (New York: N.p., 1962), 133.
10. The Inspiring Journal, theinspiringjournal.com.
11. Andrew Carnegie, *Autobiography of Andrew Carnegie* (Boston: N.p., 1920), 6.
12. Carnegie, *Gospel of Wealth*.

Chapter 2

13. O'Donnell, "America in the Gilded Age."

14. Ibid., 47.

15. Jone Johnson Lewis, "Sorosis," ThoughtCo, March 7, 2017, thoughtco. com.

16. Ibid.

17. Julia A. Sprague. *History of the New England Women's Club from 1868 to 1893* (Boston: N.p., Lee & Shepard, 1894).

18. Ibid.

19. McGerr, *Fierce Discontent*, 53.

20. Carla Eilo, "It's Our History: Lake Placid's Home Economics History," *Lake Placid News*, November 17, 2016.

21. Ibid.

22. McGerr, *Fierce Discontent*, 42.

Chapter 3

23. Tony Moore, Jacob Riis Biography website, A&E Television Networks, November 2015; Kaplan, *Lillian Wald*.

24. Moore, Jacob Riis Biography.

25. Kaplan, *Lillian Wald*.

26. Jack Rogers and Robin Blade, "The Great Ends of the Church: Two Perspectives," *Journal of Presbyterian History* 76, no. 3 (1998): 181–86.

27. Stanley Kutler, ed., "Social Gospel," in *Dictionary of American History*, vol. 7 (New York: Thomson Gale, 2003).

Chapter 4

28. Madison Horne, "Photos Reveal Shocking Conditions of Tenement Slums in Late 1800s," History, January 22, 2020, history.com.

29. gvshp.org/_gvshp/preservation/south_village/doc/SVDolkartReport. pdf.

30. Sarah Bean Apmann, "Tenement House Act of 1901," *Off the Grid* (blog), Village Preservation, April 11, 2016, http://gvshp.org.

31. McGerr, *Fierce Discontent*, 105.

Chapter 5

32. Ibid., 107.
33. Kaplan, *Lillian Wald*.
34. Ibid.
35. Lillian Wald, *The House on Henry Street* (New York: Henry Holt and Company, 1915), 135.
36. Ibid.

Chapter 6

37. Taylor Street Archives, taylorstreetarchives.com.
38. Barbara Garland Polikoff, *With One Bold Act: The Story of Jane Addams* (New York: Boswell Books, 1999), 124–26.
39. Beatrice Siegel, *Lillian Wald of Henry Street* (New York: Macmillan, 1983), 16.
40. Kaplan, *Lillian Wald*.
41. Siegel, *Lillian Wald*, 26.
42. Kaplan, *Lillian Wald*.
43. "The Progressive Era," Lumen, courses.lumenlearning.com.

Chapter 7

44. Ibid.
45. Ibid.
46. "George Washington's $300,000 Library Book Fine," BBC, news.bbc.co.uk.
47. Burns, *New York*.
48. Russell Sanjek, *American Popular Music and Its Business: The First Four Hundred Years* (New York: Oxford University Press, 1988).
49. McGerr, *Fierce Discontent*, 251.
50. Ibid., 253.
51. Allan Mazur, "U.S Trends in Feminine Beauty and Over-Adaptation," *Journal of Sex Research* 22, no. 3 (August 1986): 288.
52. Martha Patterson, *Beyond the Gibson Girl: Re-imagining the American New Woman* 1895–1915. (Chicago: University of Illinois Press, 2008).
53. "Why Do They Call Me a Gibson Girl? Miss Camille Clifford Singing the Song Which Reached Miss Edna May's Heart," *Bystander* 12, no. 149 (October 10, 1906): 83.

54. McGerr, *Fierce Discontent*, 64
55. Ibid., 263.

Chapter 8

56. Crain, *Gilded Age*, 240
57. Ida Harper, *The History of Woman Suffrage Movement*, vol. 6 (New York: NAWSA, 1922), 459–60.
58. Brooke Kroeger, *The Suffragents: How Women Used Men to Get the Vote* (Albany: SUNY Press, 2017), 1.
59. Harriot Blatch, *Challenging Years: The Memoirs of Harriot Stanton Blatch* (New York: G.P. Putnam's Sons, 1940).
60. Papers of Woodrow Wilson 40, 196, "After Dinner Speech to the Gridiron Club," December 9, 1916.
61. Turning Point, "November 17, 1917," Suffragistmemorial.org.
62. Ibid., taken from original notes and reporter coverage of the Cooper Union meeting.
63. "Talk of Dropping Capital Pickets," *New York Times*, November 9, 1917.
64. Ibid.
65. "Wilson Backs Amendment for Woman Suffrage," *New York Times*, January 10, 1918, as cited in Kroeger, *Suffragents*, 238.
66. Anne Scott and Andrew MacKay Scott, *One Half the People: The Fight for Woman Suffrage* (Champaign: University of Illinois Press, 1982), as cited in Kroeger, *Suffragents*, 240.
67. Kroeger, *Suffragents*, 238.

Chapter 9

68. McGerr, *Fierce Discontent*, 196.
69. Ibid., 215.
70. Michael Blanding, "The Racism of the Progressive Era," Princeton Alumni Weekly, paw.princeton.edu.
71. Ibid.
72. Equal Justice Initiative, "Lynching in America: Confronting the Legacy of Racial Terror," https://lynchinginamerica.eji.org/report.
73. Lorraine B. Diehl, *The Late, Great Pennsylvania Station* (New York: Four Walls, Eight Windows, 1996), 71.

74. Documents of the Assembly of the State of New York, vol. 4.

75. Paul Kaplan, *New York's Original Penn Station: The Rise and Fall of an American Landmark* (Charleston, SC: The History Press, 2019).

76. Amisha Padnani and Veronica Chambers, "Overlooked," *New York Times*, January 31, 2019.

Chapter 10

77. David Montgomery, *Fall of the House of Labor* (Cambridge: Cambridge University Press, 2005.) 207–13.

78. Philip Foner, *Organized Labor and the Black Worker, 1619–1981* (Chicago: Haymarket Books, 1982).

79. Ibid.

80. Ibid.

81. Ibid.

82. McGerr, *Fierce Discontent*, 136.

83. *Muller v. Oregon.*

84. Judith Baer, *Chains of Protection: The Judicial Response to Women's Labor Legislation* (Santa Barbara, CA: ABC-CLIO, LLC, 1978), 49–50; John Commons, *History of Labour in the United States*, (New York: Macmillan, 1918), 672–73.

85. McGerr, *Fierce Discontent*,137.

86. Ibid., 132.

87. Commons, *History of Labour.*

88. Samuel Gompers, *Seventy Years of Life and Labor* (New York: E.P. Dutton & Company, 1925), 32–34.

89. Burns, *New York.*

90. Wald, *House on Henry Street*, 209.

91. Kaplan, *Lillian Wald.*

92. Cornell University, politicalcorrection.org.

93. Ibid., 133.

94. Jane Addams, "The Settlement as a Factor in the Labor Movement," in *Residents of Hull House, Hull House Maps and Papers* (New York: N.p., 1895) 183–204.

95. McGerr, *Fierce Discontent*,137.

Chapter 11

96. Ibid., 154.
97. Ibid., 161.

Chapter 13

98. George Washington Plunkitt, *Plunkitt of Tammany Hall: A Series of Very Plain Talks on Very Practical Politics*, ed. William Riordon (New York: N.p., 1948), 37.
99. Charles Gardner, *Doctor and the Devil* (New York: N.p., 1894), 44.
100. "Gardner and Parkhurst," *New York Times*, February 10, 1893.
101. Zacks, *Island of Vice*, 87.
102. E.L. Godkin, *Triumph of Reform* (N.p., 1894), 126.
103. Plunkitt, *Plunkitt of Tammany Hall*, 15.
104. Lincoln Steffens, "The Real Roosevelt," *Ainslee's Magazine*, December 1898.
105. "Business, Not Politics," *New York World*, May 22, 1895.
106. National Constitution Center, "Popular Election of Senators," Interactive Constitution, Constitutioncenter.org.
107. Ibid.

Chapter 14

108. Burns, *Prohibition*.
109. Ibid.
110. John Metcalfe, "When Lager Reigned," City Lab, February 20, 2017, Citylab.com.
111. Burns, *Prohibition*.
112. Ibid.
113. Ibid.
114. Ibid.
115. Ibid.
116. Ibid.
117. Robert Graham, Church Temperance Society publications, circa early 1890s.
118. Robert Graham, "New York City and Its Masters," Church Temperance Society publication, 1887.

119. Ibid.
120. Henry William Blair, *The Temperance Movement, or the Conflict Between Man & Alcohol* (Boston: William Smythe Company, 1888).
121. Joseph Pollard, *The Road to Repeal: Submission to Conventions* (New York: Brentano's, 1932).
122. Austin Kerr, *Organized for Prohibition: A New History of the Anti-Saloon League* (New Haven, CT: Yale University Press, 1985).
123. "Prohibition," Digital History, Digitalhistory.uh.edu.
124. Burns, *Prohibition*.
125. McGerr, *Fierce Discontent*, 93.

Chapter 15

126. Virginia Scharff, *Taking the Wheel: Women and the Coming of the Motor Age* (Albuquerque: University of New Mexico Press, 1992).
127. Diehl, 65.
128. Jill Jonnes, *Conquering Gotham: Building Penn Station and Its Tunnels* (New York: Penguin Books, 2008) 26.
129. Kaplan, *New York's Original Penn Station*.

Chapter 16

130. "Theodore Roosevelt," PBS, pbs.org.
131. Ibid.
132. Ibid.
133. Humane Society of New York, http://www.humanesocietyny.org.
134. Ibid.

Chapter 17

135. Snag Films, guidebookstgc.snagfilms.com/8535_America_GildedAge.pdf.

BIBLIOGRAPHY

Books

Brooks, Thomas. *Toil and Trouble: A History of American Labor*. New York: Delacorte Press, 1971.

Cantor, Milton. *The Divided Left: American Radicalism, 1900–1975*. New York: Hill and Wang, 1978.

Crain, Esther. *The Gilded Age in New York*. New York: Black Dog and Leventhal Publishers, 2016.

Graham, Robert. *New York City and Its Masters*. N.p.: Church Temperance Society, 1887.

Kroeger, Brooke. *The Suffragents: How Women Used Men to Get the Vote*. Albany, NY: SUNY Press, 2017.

McGerr, Michael. *A Fierce Discontent: The Rise and Fall of the Progressive Movement in America*. New York: Oxford University Press, 2003.

Zacks, Richard. *Island of Vice: Theodore Roosevelt's Doomed Quest to Clean Up Sin-Loving New York*. New York: Doubleday, 2012.

Documentaries

Burns, Ken, and Lynn Novick. *Prohibition*. PBS, October 2, 2011.

Burns, Ric. *New York: A Documentary Film*. PBS, November 14, 1999.

BIBLIOGRAPHY

Teaching Series

O'Donnell, Edward T. "America in the Gilded Age and Progressive Era."
Great Courses. Course Number 8535, 2015.

Museum Exhibits

Ford Piquette Avenue Plant. Detroit, Michigan.
Henry Ford Museum. Dearborn, Michigan.
Tenement Museum. Lower East Side, New York.

Short Essays

Jackson Lears, T. "The Guilded Age." Gilder Lehrman Institute of American
History. ap.gilderlehrman.org.

Articles

Blanding, Michael. "The Racism of the Progressive Era." *Princeton Alumni
Weekly*, March 1, 2017.

Poetry Collection

Wolf, Stephen, ed. *I Speak of the City: Poems of New York*. New York: Columbia
University Press, 2007.

Web Sites

City Lab. Citylab.com.
Greenwich Village Society for Historic Preservation (blog). Gvshp.org.
History. History.com
Humane Society of New York. http://www.humanesocietyny.org.
Princeton Alumni Weekly. Paw.princeton.edu.
Public Broadcasting Service. PBS.org.

INDEX

About the Author

Paul Kaplan writes critically acclaimed books in three series: cultural guides (*Jewish New York: A History and Guide to Neighborhoods, Synagogues, & Eateries* and *Jewish South Florida*), social history and biography (*New York's Original Penn Station: The Rise and Tragic Fall of an American Landmark, Lillian Wald: America's Great Social and Healthcare Reformer* and a children's book on Irving Berlin) and business marketing (*Content Marketing for Success: Build Your Brand and Generate Leads*). He has been featured on numerous radio shows, including *Woodstock Booktalk, America's Dining & Travel, Let's Travel Radio* and *Writer's Voice*. His books have been on PBS-WNET and CBS Miami. He's been featured in several newspapers and magazines, including the *New York Press, Princeton Magazine, Amsterdam New York* and *Reminisce* magazine. He gives book tours to several organizations at venues throughout the United States. Kaplan earned a bachelor of arts in ethics, politics and economics from Yale College and a master's of business administration from the Yale School of Management. Kaplan maintains a career as a marketing director for the publishing, technology, educational and financial industries. His website is paulkaplanauthor.com.

Visit us at
www.historypress.com